The New York Times

SO-EIL-029

CHANGING PERSPECTIVES

Women's Roles

THE NEW YORK TIMES EDITORIAL STAFF

Published in 2019 by New York Times Educational Publishing
in association with The Rosen Publishing Group, Inc.
29 East 21st Street, New York, NY 10010

Contains material from The New York Times and is reprinted
by permission. Copyright © 2019 The New York Times.
All rights reserved.

Rosen Publishing materials copyright © 2019 The Rosen
Publishing Group, Inc. All rights reserved. Distributed
exclusively by Rosen Publishing.

First Edition

The New York Times
Alex Ward: Editorial Director, Book Development
Brenda Hutchings: Senior Photo Editor/Art Buyer
Phyllis Collazo: Photo Rights/Permissions Editor
Heidi Giovine: Administrative Manager

Rosen Publishing
Greg Tucker: Creative Director
Brian Garvey: Art Director
Megan Kellerman: Managing Editor
Danielle Weiner: Editor

Cataloging-in-Publication Data
Names: New York Times Company.
Title: Women's roles / edited by the New York Times editorial staff.
Description: New York : The New York Times Educational Publishing,
2019. | Series: Changing perspectives | Includes glossary and index.
Identifiers: ISBN 9781642820706 (pbk.) | ISBN 9781642820690
(library bound) | ISBN 9781642820683 (ebook)
Subjects: LCSH: Women—United States—Social conditions—
Juvenile literature. | Women's rights—Juvenile literature. |
Women—Employment—Juvenile literature. | Women—Political
activity—United States—Juvenile literature. | Women politicians—
United States—Juvenile literature.
Classification: LCC HQ1418.W664 2019 | DDC 305.40973—dc23

Manufactured in the United States of America

On the cover: Illustration by Franziska Barczyk.

Contents

CHAPTER 3

At Work

CHAPTER 4

In Politics

CHAPTER 5

Society, Sex and Relationships

Introduction

WHAT IS A woman's role in society? It depends on who you ask — and when. Perspectives about women's roles are more than just opinions. They influence the rules and expectations for how women conduct their lives, relationships, and intellectual pursuits. A look at the newspaper coverage over the past 150 years shows that much has changed for women in the United States. It also shows how difficult it is to change public opinion even over long periods of time. Remnants of decades-old viewpoints about women's rights and roles infuse the mind-sets and laws debated today.

Beliefs about women's roles change primarily through two channels: legislation and social norms. These affect each other, but not necessarily at the same time. Until the middle of the 19th century, a woman's primary role was homemaker. Women were not encouraged to pursue formal education, but rather to prepare for life as wives. Once married, women no longer had the right to own property or keep their wages. They could not sign contracts and did not have the right to vote. Many women chafed at these restrictions, and some decided to advocate for change.

The fight for women's rights in the United States began in 1848 at a convention in Seneca Falls, New York. There, the Declaration of Sentiments was issued, proposing an end to discrimination against women. By 1900, every state in the nation had passed legislation allowing married women to have some control over their property and income.

Margaret Sanger opened the country's first birth control clinic in Brooklyn, New York, in 1916. She was arrested for running a "public nuisance" and imprisoned for 30 days. Two years later, she won a lawsuit that enabled doctors to educate all patients — not just the wealthy

ALYSSA SCHUKAR FOR THE NEW YORK TIMES

In celebration of the spirit of resistance, Women's March Chicago held "March to the Polls" in January 2018 to urge women to vote.

ones — about birth control. Although initial public opinion was that birth control education was obscene, Mrs. Sanger's trial helped to build broad social acceptance for the birth-control movement. This, in turn, paved the way for women to have more control over their sexual and reproductive lives.

Although legislation can address discrimination in pay and employment, it cannot necessarily adjust social expectations about them. Congress passed the 19th amendment, granting women the right to vote, in 1919. Three-fourths of the states ratified it in 1920. Many women turned out to vote, but few ran for electoral office until the 1970s. The Equal Pay Act was passed in 1963, but women still earn 18 percent less than men. This is often attributed to women taking time off to raise and care for children or other family members at the expense of promotions and pay raises.

Today, women are encouraged to "have it all" — a family, a home, and a successful career. But striking a balance between these demanding endeavors can prove difficult. Many women struggle with guilt, time management, and the fear of failure. Those who choose one lifestyle over the other risk alienation — and sometimes derision — from women who straddle both worlds. For some women, "having it all" is unattainable. For others, it is undesirable. But social norms today dictate that every woman should try.

Over time, women have challenged traditional beliefs about their sexuality and relationships. Flappers eschewed the social conventions of the 1920s entirely, choosing instead to drink, dance, listen to jazz, and engage openly in sexual relationships. The sexual revolution of the late 20th century expanded to include women across all social strata, and led to the general acceptance of sex outside of marriage.

A growing awareness about date rape and sexual harassment in the 1980s and 1990s gave rise to a new focus for feminism that is today heightened by the #MeToo movement. Activists are urging politicians to consider how legislation can be changed to make it more effective in combatting sexual assault. And women are running for political office to ensure that these changes are made.

As with any change, however, there has been backlash to the shifts in women's roles. There was strong resistance to the idea that women were capable of informed voting, enjoying the intellectual stimulation of higher education and working for profit or pleasure. The public questioned deeply the notion of a woman vice president, and later, a woman president. And a largely sexually-liberated society has had to grapple with the challenge of defining sexual consent.

As feminism gains traction once again, the movement strives for a broader understanding of women's roles now and what they could be, the tools necessary to shape public discourse around them and what rights and freedom for women mean in the 21st century.

CHAPTER 1

Equal by Law

The fight for equality for women is multifaceted and on-going. Over the past 150 years, women have won the legal right to own property, vote, be paid for work done outside the home and be paid wages commensurate to those of men. The fight for equality continues as activists turn their attention to sexual harassment and closing the pay gap.

Woman's Rights

BY THE NEW YORK TIMES | OCT. 18, 1851

WOMAN'S RIGHTS — We regret to see how obstinately our American women are bent on appropriating more than their fair share of Constitutional privileges. Not that the effort ever amounts to anything more than the re-affirmation of certain arrant heresies — such, for instance, as the equality of God-denying Martineau, and her black tabby — with Fame and Priestley, and others of the masculine stripe; the community of intellectual wealth between the sexes; the preponderance, if any there be, in favor of the softer of the twain; the propriety of induing their delicate forms with the apparel, appurtenances, and insignia of manhood. But there is an obvious tendency to encroach upon masculine manners, manifested even in trifles, which cannot be too severely rebuked, or too speedily repressed. We are clearly of opinion that the time has come for the organization of a "Rights of Man Association," to withstand the greedy, appropriativeness of womankind; and if that does not serve, we must resort to dissolution or secession. Anti-masculine agitation must be stayed by some means.

Women's Rights Convention.

BY THE NEW YORK TIMES | JUNE 5, 1852

WEST CHESTER, PA., THURSDAY, JUNE 3 — The Convention met at 9 o'clock.

The Business Committee reported, for the consideration of the Convention, a series of resolutions, congratulating the world on the advance made in the doctrines held by the Convention; denying the right of Legislatures to endow institutions whose advantages women were precluded from enjoying; asking for an alteration of the laws, whereby the wife may inherit the estate of her husband as he inherits hers, and be regarded as the guardian of her child; and demanding that remuneration for equal service may be the same to women as men.

The consideration of these resolutions was postponed for the present, to hear a letter read from Mary Mott, of Indiana, and to allow Ann Preston to give an exposition of the views of the Convention.

The address sets forth that women demand an equality before the law; that the property of the husband should descend to the wife, as his only heir; that women should be permitted to hold offices of trust and profit; and so trained to unfold her nature, that every path should be regarded as her appropriate sphere, wherever duty pointed.

These views were ably maintained by Mrs. Nichols, Mrs. Gage, Mrs. Rose, and Lucretia Mott, and adopted as the sentiments of the Convention.

The resolutions of the Committee were taken up, pending the discussion on which, the Convention adjourned until 2 ½ o'clock.

AFTERNOON SESSION.

The Convention met at 2 ½ o'clock, and resumed the consideration of the resolutions reported during the morning. Interesting remarks were made by B. Rush Plumly, Mrs. Gage, Mrs. Rose, and Mrs. Nichols.

Mrs. Nichols maintained that the slow advancement of all reforms heretofore, was owing to the want of women's personal cooperation, and predicted that in less than ten years women would be free.

A Committee was appointed to advance the legal and political rights of women, by preparing and circulating petitions, and acting in such other way as might be necessary.

Alter appointing a Committee on Publication, the Convention adjourned at 5 o'clock, *sine die.*

Legislation for Women.

BY THE NEW YORK TIMES | AUG. 18, 1857

THE ADVOCATES OF Women's Rights have not abandoned their cause as a hopeless one, but are still prosecuting it with increasing energy and vigor. Conventions are coming to be somewhat out of fashion, at least in the east, but other and more effective measures are being taken to equalize the property laws relating to the sexes, as well as to obtain the final ultimatum — the right of suffrage for women. In pursuance of a resolution adopted at the National Convention held in New-York last November, memorials were presented to the Legislatures of the several states during their last Winter's session, which elicited considerable discussion and some final action.

Owing to some mistake, the memorial presented the New-York Legislature was received at too late a date to receive attention.

The Legislature of Maine passed an act by which husband is entitled to an allowance in the personal estate of his deceased wife, with a distributive share in the residue thereof, in the same manner as the wife is in the estate of her husband. If she leaves issue, he has the use of one-third, if no issue, of one-half of her real estate for his life, which is received and assigned in the manner and with the rights of dower. An act was also passed, giving married women the right to their wages for services performed for other than their own family, independently of the control of their husbands.

The Legislature of Missouri passed an act providing that if a married woman be compelled, through the desertion or profligacy of her husband, to provide for the maintenance of herself and family, she shall be entitled to her own earnings, and to all real or personal property purchased therewith, and that such property shall not be liable for the debts of her husband, nor subject to his control.

A similar bill was passed by the Legislature of Indiana.

The Legislature of Ohio passed a bill enacting that no married man shall dispose of any personal property without having first obtained the consent of his wife, the wife being empowered, in case or the violation of such act, to commence a civil suit in her own name for the recovery of said property; and, also that any married woman whose husband shall desert her or neglect to provide for his family, shall be entitled to her wages and to those of her minor children. These amendments were warmly recommended by Gov. Chase in his annual message.

The Select Committee of the Senate on the petition asking the light of suffrage, reported in favor of the proposed amendment; but the bill was defeated in the Senate by a vote of 44 to 44. The petition received some ten thousand signatures.

The Select Committee of the Michigan Senate also reported favorably on a similar petition, and recommended an amendment to the Constitution, granting the right of the elective franchise to all citizens, irrespective of sex. This resolution was defeated in the Senate by a vote of 15 yeas to 17 nays, every Senator being present.

A strong report in favor of granting the right of suffrage to women was also submitted to the Senate of Wisconsin by the Committee appointed to report thereon, but with similar success.

We understand that effective and well-organized efforts will be made during the ensuing Winter to bring the subject before the Legislatures of the different States.

John P. Hale on Women's Rights.

BY THE NEW YORK TIMES | JULY 17, 1858

JOHN P. HALE, of New Hampshire, made a speech on Tuesday to the graduating Class of the Abbott Female Academy, at Andover, in which he gave then his views of the Women's Rights question:

> "The present day had afforded to us many proofs that science was not confined to men — as for instance, Miss Mitchell, the astronomer. Mathematics were also open to women. 'Let me write the songs of a nation, and I care not who makes the laws,' was a saying of deep import; the poetic fields were open to women. So in all the other higher branches of knowledge. Now there were some who did not believe women would have all their rights till they had the right of suffrage. But if this right were obtained it might be found to degrade, instead of elevating female life. What was there in the exercise of the right to suffrage to produce moral elevation? We did not see that the men in cities who exercised the right were ennobled, refined or elevated by going to the ballot box. Every female of delicacy must revolt at finding herself in contaminating contact with the influences of the polls; as she would thereby be placed in conflict and on a level with every blackguard. Female influence was not silent to-day in controlling the politics of the country. An eminent gentleman had said that if he wished to control a canvass for the good of a State, he would sooner address the children and young women than the men. As women trained their sons and brothers, so would the future voters of the country be. Each woman would probably have at least one willing friend, who would be ready to consult her opinions."

A lady friend had asked him what she should do as she was deprived of the right of voting, and he told her to go and unite her fortunes with one whose right to vote was unquestioned, [laughter,] and thereupon she had told him that was the meanest thing he had ever said. Those unfortunate females who were always complaining of their limited spheres, would be found to be those who had not the courage and faith and energy to do what was even in that limited sphere for them. No one had a right to complain so long as in the sphere of their influence they had left a single duty unperformed. Not until we had done what we could should we sit down with Alexander and cry that there were no more worlds to conquer. We should not complain while a single case of human wretchedness existed which we had not done what we could to alleviate by sympathy or aid.

In addressing young ladies, he could not present the same motives which were usual in addressing boys, but he could assure them that every one could obtain all the good in life which they deserved. In concluding, Mr. Hale told a story of a young girl, who said she had two things settled in her own mind; first, she would never marry a minister; second, she would never live in the town of B. Yet, she eventually married a minister of B.

"So it will be with you, my young friends," said Mr Hale to the young ladies, at which great laughter and clapping ensued. "I perceive," continued he, "that it is the theological students that are clapping, because they think you will all marry ministers." [Renewed merriment.] But the moral of all he had said to-day was that the same duty pertained to all. Instead of sitting down and sighing over the allotments of our condition, we should each meet and discharge with zeal, energy and faith, the duties of the position in which we severally found ourselves.

Suffrage Wins in the Senate;
Now Goes to States

BY THE NEW YORK TIMES | JUNE 5, 1919

WASHINGTON, JUNE 4 — After a long and persistent fight advocates of women suffrage won a victory in the Senate today when that body, by a vote of 56 to 25, adopted the Susan Anthony amendment to the Constitution. The suffrage supporters had two more than the necessary two-thirds vote of Senators present. Had all the Senators known to be in favor of suffrage been present the amendment would have had 66 votes, or two more than a two-thirds vote of the entire Senate.

The amendment, having already been passed by the House, where the vote was 304 to 80, now goes to the States for ratification, where it will be passed upon in the form in which it has been adopted by Congress, as follows:

> *"Article —, Section. — The right of citizens of the United States to vote shall not be denied or abridged by the United States or by any State on account of sex.*
>
> *"Section 2. — Congress shall have power, by appropriate legislation, to enforce the provisions of this article."*

Leaders of the National Women's Party announced tonight that they would at once embark upon a campaign to obtain ratification of the amendment by the necessary three-fourths of the States so that women might have the vote in the next Presidential election. To achieve this ratification it will be necessary to hold special sessions of some Legislatures which otherwise would not convene until after the Presidential election in 1920. Miss Alice Paul, Chairman of the Woman's Party, predicted that the campaign for ratification would succeed and that women would vote for the next President.

Suffragists thronged the Senate galleries in anticipation of the final vote, and when the outcome was announced by President Pro Tem. Cummins they broke into deafening applause. For two minutes the demonstration went on, Senator Cummins making no effort to check it.

The vote came after four hours of debate during which Democratic Senators opposed to the amendment filibustered to prevent a roll call until their absent Senators could be protected by pairs. They gave up the effort finally as futile.

CHANGES DEFEATED.

Before the final vote was taken Senator Underwood of Alabama called for vote on his amendment to submit the suffrage amendment to Constitutional conventions of the various States, instead of to the Legislatures, for ratification. This was defeated by a vote of 55 against to 28 in favor.

Senator Gay of Louisiana offered an amendment proposing enforcement of the suffrage amendment by the States, instead of by the Federal Government. Senator Gay said that from a survey of the States he could predict that thirteen states would not ratify the amendment, enough to block it. His amendment was defeated, 62 to 19.

During debate, Senator Wadsworth of New York, who has been an uncompromising opponent of women suffrage, explained his attitude as being actuated by the motive of preserving to the States the right to determine the question, each State for itself.

"No vote of mine cast upon this amendment would deprive any of the lectors of my State of any privilege they now enjoy," said the Senator. "I feel so strongly that the people of the several States should be permitted to decide for themselves that I am frank to say, that, if this amendment, instead of being drafted to extend woman suffrage all over the country, were drafted to forbid the extension of the franchise to women in the States, I would vote against it. Even though one might be opposed on general principles to the extension of the franchise to women, one cannot logically object to the people of a State settling that question for themselves.

"It seems to me that it is incumbent upon a Senator in considering his attitude on this matter to regard the nation as a whole and to give consideration to the wishes of the people of the various States which have expressed themselves from time to time."

OVERRIDING STATE VOTES

Senator Wadsworth spoke of the results in Massachusetts, New Jersey, Pennsylvania, West Virginia, Ohio, Louisiana, Texas, Wisconsin, and other States where women suffrage was defeated at the polls.

"Now the question is," he resumed, "whether the people of these States are competent to settle the question for themselves. There is no tremendous emergency facing the country, no revolution or rebellion threatened, which would seem to make it necessary to impose on the people of these States a thing they have said as free citizens they do not require or desire. It is contrary to the spirit of American institutions that they shall be left free to decide these things for themselves?

"My contention has been, with respect to an amendment to the Constitution, that, if it be placed there, it should command the reverence and devotion of all the people of the country. The discussion here yesterday makes it perfectly apparent that, in part at least, in a certain section of this country, this proposed amendment will be a dead letter. No pretense is made that it will be lived up to in spirit as well as in letter. That same attitude has been manifest in the discussion of the last amendment to the Constitution, ratified last Winter. Today there are thousands of people all over the United States who are attempting to contrive ways by which the prohibition amendment can be evaded. This attitude shows an utter lack of appreciation of the Constitution as a sacred instrument, a lack of realization of the spirit of self-government."

Senator Smith of South Carolina opposed giving women the right to vote, he said, because to allow it would induce "sectional anarchy."

SIGNING OF THE RESOLUTION.

Immediately after its passage by the Senate the Suffrage Amendment was signed. In appreciation of the fifty-year campaign of the National American Woman Suffrage Association, the guests were limited to representatives of that association and members of Congress, and the gold pen used was presented to the national association. The women chosen to represent the national association were Mrs. Wood Park of Massachusetts, who for two years has been in charge of the association's Congressional work; Mrs. Helen Gardener of Washington, D. C.; Mrs. Ida Husted Harper of New York, Mrs. Harriet Taylor Upton of Ohio, Miss Mary G. Hay, and Miss Marjorie Shuler of New York.

Besides Speaker Gillett, who signed the bill, the members of the House present were Frank W. Mondell, majority leader; Champ Clark, minority leader and ex-Speaker, under whom the amendment first passed the House, and John E. Raker, Chairman of the committee which won the suffrage victory in the House last year.

The Senators present at the signing of the bill for the Senate were Albert B. Cummins, President Pro Tempore, who signed the measure; James E. Watson, Chairman of the Suffrage Committee; Charles Curtis, Republican whip; A. A. Jones, Chairman of the Suffrage Committee in the last Congress; Thomas J. Walsh of Montana, Morris Sheppard, Joseph E. Ransdell, and Reed Smoot.

To celebrate the passage of the amendment the national association will give a reception next Tuesday evening at its Washington headquarters to the members of the House and Senate who voted for the resolution and to their wives. These will be the only guests.

Miss Paul, Chairman of the National Woman's Party, issued a statement, in which she said: "There is no doubt of ratification by the States. We enter upon the campaign for special sessions of Legislatures to accomplish this ratification before 1920 in the full assurance that we shall win."

"The last stage of the fight is to obtain ratification of the amendment so women may vote in the Presidential election in 1920," said Mrs. Carrie Chapman Catt, President of the association. "This we are confident will be achieved. The friends of woman suffrage in both parties have carried out their word. In the result we can turn our backs upon the end of a long and arduous struggle, needlessly darkened and embittered by the stubbornness of a few at the expense of the many. 'Eyes front' is the watchword as we turn upon the struggle for ratification by the States."

PROSPECTS OF RATIFICATION.

Suffrage leaders say quick ratification is assured in twenty-eight States in which women now have full or Presidential suffrage. These States are Wyoming, Colorado, Utah, Idaho, Washington, California, Kansas, Arizona, Oregon, Montana, New York, Oklahoma, South Dakota, Michigan, Illinois, Nebraska, Rhode Island, North Dakota, Iowa, Wisconsin, Indiana, Maine, Minnesota, Missouri, Tennessee, Arkansas, Nevada, and Texas.

Legislatures now in session are: Illinois, will adjourn late in June; Pennsylvania, Massachusetts, adjourn end of June or first of July; Wisconsin, Florida, in session until June 1, cannot ratify because an election must intervene between submission of amendment and ratification.

Legislatures to meet comparatively soon, or with prospects of meeting soon, are: Michigan and Texas, extra sessions called in June; Georgia, to meet this month; Alabama, to meet in July; Louisiana, possibility of extra session before September; New Jersey, movement for extra session soon; Maine, special session in October; Iowa, special session in January; Kentucky, South Carolina and Mississippi, meet in January; Virginia, meets in February; Maryland, meets during 1920; Ohio, meets in June.

Today's victory for suffrage ends a fight that really dates from the American Revolution. Women voted under several of the Colonial Governments. During the Revolution women demanded to be included in the Government. Abigail Adams wrote her husband, John Adams, "If women are not represented in this new republic there will be another revolution." From the time of the Revolution women agitated for suffrage by means of meetings and petitions. In 1848 a woman's rights convention was held at Seneca Falls, N. Y., arranged by Lucretia Mott and Elizabeth Cady Stanton as the first big suffrage demonstration. From 1848 to the civil war efforts were made to have State laws altered to include women, and Susan B. Anthony became the leader of the movement.

For five years after the civil war suffragists tried to secure interpretation of the Fourteenth and Fifteenth Amendments which would permit them to vote. In 1872 Miss Anthony made a test vote at the polls, was arrested, and refused to pay her fine, but was never jailed. In 1875 Miss Anthony drafted the proposed Federal amendment, the same one that was voted on today. In 1878 the amendment was introduced in the Senate by Senator Sargent of California. It has been voted on in the Senate five times, including today. In 1878 the vote was 16 yeas to 34 nays; in 1914 it failed by 11 votes, in 1918 it failed by two votes, and on Feb. 10, 1919, it failed by one vote. It has been voted on three times in the House. It failed there in 1915 by 78 votes. In 1918 it passed the House with 14 votes more than the necessary two-thirds.

Foreign countries or divisions of countries in which women have suffrage are: Isle of Man, granted 1881; New Zealand, 1893; Australia, 1902; Finland, 1906; Norway, 1907; Iceland, 1913; Denmark, 1915; Russia, 1917; Canada, Austria, England, Germany, Hungary, Ireland, Poland, Scotland, and Wales, 1918; Holland and Sweden, 1919.

On Equal Rights for Women

BY THE NEW YORK TIMES | SEPT. 12, 1964

WASHINGTON, SEPT. 11 — The Senate Judiciary Committee approved today a proposed "equal rights for women" amendment to the Constitution.

It provides that "equality of rights under the law shall not be denied or abridged by the United States or by any state on account of sex."

The committee has favorably reported the proposed amendment in seven previous Congresses, but it never has been passed by both the Senate and the House.

Call to Action

BY THE NEW YORK TIMES | MARCH 24, 1972

IN PASSING A Constitutional amendment assuring equal rights for women, Congress has at last done what, principle, it should have done long ago. In spite of oft expressed reservations about the amendment's oversim plified form, we are glad of its approval and hope it will enjoy swift ratification by the states.

The reservations of this newspaper, and of many other libertarian institutions and individuals, were at no time directed to the measure's basic purpose — the absolute right of women to freedom from economic, political and legal discrimination on the basis of sex. What worried U.S. was the risk that, in the name of equality, women might be deprived of health and safety protections which may be of small consequence to professional promoters of a good cause but which can and do make a grave difference in the daily lives of women workers in shops and factories.

Those are still important considerations, and we wish Congress had not dealt so lightly with attempts to take them into account. Similarly, the possible eligibility women for the military draft (including combat duty), given the broad language of the amendment, is a question that surely deserved more than the cavalier brush-off it received on Capitol Hill. Had women, from all walks of life, made up a majority of the Congress, it is a fair bet that the entire subject would have had more intelligent and searching examination than it got from a male majority touched with guilt and politically cagey.

Now that the amendment is on its way to ratification by the states, we earnestly hope that our specific concerns prove groundless. Discrimination against women has disfigured almost every aspect of American life. Congressional approval of this repudiation of such injustice should and must become a national call to action.

2 Approaches to Rebuilding Women's Movement

BY JULIE JOHNSON | AUG. 14, 1989

SEIZING AN OPPORTUNITY created by the Supreme Court's recent abortion ruling, two research groups are hoping to help foster a renewal of activism in the women's movement and infuse it with a sense of mission.

What it means to be feminist, especially to younger women, will be the focus of a conference planned in November by the Center for Women Policy Studies and another one next summer by the Institute for Women's Policy Research.

Adopting different approaches, the Washington-based organizations will seek to stimulate a search by women for new political and legislative strategies to win economic and political gains that have eluded them in the last decade. Both groups are aiming at women who are 18 to 29 years old, those who were in diapers or not yet born when Betty Friedan first identified the "feminine mystique" in 1963 and propelled women's concerns into the national conscience.

'EMBARRASSED' FEMINISTS

Although the Court's decision upholding restrictions on abortions "is galvanizing young women," said Mara Verheyden-Hilliard, project director for the November conference, many of these women remain "embarrassed to say they are feminists, often because of the connotations people use to define feminism."

The Center for Women Policy Studies, a research group established in 1972, is bringing together older feminists with younger women who feel comfortable with that label and are looking to expand upon it. Its conference will focus heavily on reproductive rights.

'BACK TO THE MAINSTREAM'

On the other hand, the two-year-old Institute for Women's Policy Research is designed to appeal to women who endorse many women's issues but who may not be comfortable with the feminist label. The group has not decided to what extent its conference will focus on abortion.

Sarah E. Jones, a 24-year-old legal assistant and former Congressional aide who is helping to plan the institute's conference, said that among the women who believe that feminist rhetoric should be tempered there is still a feeling that it is time to bring the movement "back to the mainstream."

Leslie R. Wolfe, the center's executive director, said women in their 20's had "a different set of perspectives and start with certain assumptions that women of my generation had to struggle to accept."

'INSTITUTIONS HAVE TO CHANGE'

"They believe we are equally capable of being parents and workers and leaders as men are, and that what has to happen — and this is the focus of the conference — is that the institutions have to change rather than the women," she said.

The center's conference, scheduled Nov. 10-12, will discuss how to "structure the work place and structure leadership in government" as well as child care, family and medical leave, abortion, education and employment.

Ms. Wolfe said planners would offer a vision of a "new feminism" spanning generations and incorporating a broad range of issues, including "racism, heterosexism, disability rights and all discrimination."

"Young women want to get a foot in the door of the movement," she said.

'DON'T HAVE TO BE RADICAL'

Ms. Jones said the institute's conference would be based on the thought that "to be feminist you don't have to be radical or a lesbian."

"There seems to be this dilemma among young women who identify with the issues and who in effect are saying, 'Don't call me a feminist but, yeah, I'm a feminist,' " she said.

While she does not shun the "feminist" label, Ms. Jones said it carried many political implications, particularly in states with smaller urban populations, like her home state of Mississippi.

Nadia Moritz, an aide at the institute and the conference's project director, said, "We want to see what young women's attitudes are about the women's movement."

Ms. Moritz, who is 25 years old, said women had begun to realize that their gains might be eroding. For cxample, she said, the Supreme Court's recent term also included decisions that limited the ability of women and other minorities to bring or win lawsuits alleging bias by an employer.

"It has made some women who haven't thought about women's issues in general now scared," said Randi Mandelbaum, a 25-year-old lawyer who is a conference planner.

OBSTACLES TO SUCCESS

But even as the Washington conferences are planned, some experts in women's affairs caution that it may be some time before large numbers of young women become openly and actively involved.

Susan M. Hartmann, a professor of women's history and director of the Center for Women's Studies at Ohio State University, said that while the Court's abortion decision had mobilized more women, "I think restrictions on abortion will have to get more severe for it to have a really enormous impact on young women."

Professor Hartmann said the women's movement had historically comprised and had been dominated by generally affluent, well-educated women. And it is among these groups that abortion is least threatened.

And, the experts said, even while many professional, college-educated women are philosophically attuned to the issues, some are too young to have experienced difficulties with child care or infertility or the elimination of barriers on the job, particularly at higher levels.

Deborah Shultz, a staff member at the National Council for Research on Women in New York and a 28-year-old graduate student in women's history, said: "I think there's a lot of denial on the part of young women about the barriers that are there and also ignorance of them until they personally hit the glass ceiling."

Guiding the Battles of the Women's Rights Movement

BY TAMAR LEWIN | DEC. 16, 2000

IT WAS SHEER woman power — secretary power, actually — that got Marcia D. Greenberger the job as the first full-time women's rights lawyer in Washington. Back in the early 1970's, the headiest days of the women's movement, the secretaries at the Center for Law and Social Policy went to the male lawyers who founded the group and presented a list of demands: They did not want to serve coffee anymore. They wanted raises. They wanted the center to start a women's rights project. And they wanted a female lawyer hired for it.

Enter Ms. Greenberger, two years out of the University of Pennsylvania law school and working, with something less than passion, as a tax lawyer in a private firm.

Her first case at the center challenged a company policy excluding pregnancy from disability coverage, and paved the way for the Pregnancy Discrimination Act — as well as Wednesday's decision by the Equal Employment Opportunity Commission that employers whose health plans cover other preventive care must also cover prescription contraceptives.

But that is skipping a quarter-century ahead of the story.

When Ms. Greenberger went to interview at the center, the male lawyers were not sure there was enough women's rights work to keep a full-time lawyer busy. She had no doubts, given the array of new federal antidiscrimination laws — and her own experiences.

"Remember, I went to law school and looked for my first job at a time when there was no law giving women any right to equal treatment," said Ms. Greenberger, now 54, in her sunny office at the National Women's Law Center, which became independent from the Center for Law and Social Policy in 1981. "In law school, it was just accepted that they called on women when they got to the rape cases."

There were about 10 women in her class of 200, she said, and they were not allowed to live in the law student's dorm. But she got to know one dorm resident very well. The class was divided alphabetically, and Marcia Devins was in the same section as Michael Greenberger: They got married after second year. Mr. Greenberger now works at the Justice Department.

At graduation, he got a clerkship with a Washington judge, but the professors discouraged her from applying for one, telling her that most judges did not take women clerks, and no one would want a woman with a husband in another judge's chambers. Many law firms were none too eager, either.

"One firm told me that they wouldn't hire women lawyers, because Washington was not a safe city, they worked late hours, and they would feel just terrible if anything happened to a young woman going home," Ms. Greenberger said in her measured, lawyerly way. "I'm still sorry that it wasn't until I was out the door that I realized I should have asked what they did for all the women who worked there as assistants."

Ms. Greenberger, who grew up in Philadelphia, was always interested in social justice and policy. "My father was a teacher and my mother, as we say now, worked in the home," she said. "They were very politically aware. I grew up watching the McCarthy hearings. And I was completely swept away by John Kennedy. When I was finishing law school, I wrote to ask about jobs on Capitol Hill. But I didn't know anyone, I didn't know anyone who knew anyone, and I didn't even know enough to know I should try to make those connections."

These days, Ms. Greenberger has connections aplenty. Starting with that first case at the center, she put together a coalition of women's groups — there were fewer then — to support a union woman challenging General Electric's exclusion of pregnancy from disability coverage.

"Pregnancy discrimination was common back then," she said. "Pregnancy, or the capacity to become pregnant, was used as a reason not to hire women, or to give them lower pay. And not only did G.E. not cover disability for the recovery period after a normal pregnancy, it didn't even pay for women who were disabled from complications of pregnancy. Men injured in skiing accidents or bar brawls got disability, but G.E. said that pregnancy was unique, so different that it wasn't covered under Title VII's prohibition of sex discrimination in the workplace."

The case went to the United States Supreme Court, which in 1976 sided with General Electric — prompting such a furor that two years later, Congress passed the Pregnancy Discrimination Act. That law, this week, was the basis for the E.E.O.C.'s ruling on contraceptive coverage. And this time, too, Ms. Greenberger had put together a coalition of women's groups, health groups and civil rights groups to press the issue, laying the groundwork for this week's decision.

"I think women now understand that the law can protect them and that their child-bearing capacity is something positive, for which they should not be penalized," Ms. Greenberger said. "Women's rights have come a long way."

Of course, Ms. Greenberger and her causes have their critics. Business groups say that her efforts to mandate new insurance coverage costs too much and the Catholic Church and others who oppose abortion are natural opponents.

And while her two daughters — Sarah, teaching in the Bronx, and Anne, in college at her parents' alma mater, Penn — have broader opportunities than she did, Ms. Greenberger says, the job is by no means finished.

"We have to be very vigilant to defend the rights we've won," said Ms. Greenberger, who for two decades has shared the co-presidency of the Center with Duffy Campbell, an arrangement that lets both women do substantive law and administrative work.

The center now has a staff of 39, including 22 lawyers and — Ms. Greenberger admits shamefacedly — only one man.

He is a secretary? "Administrative assistant," she said.

How Should We Respond to Sexual Harassment?

BY AMANDA TAUB | NOV. 29, 2017

AS ACCUSATIONS OF sexual misconduct against famous men accumulate, the sheer quantity of dispiriting news is starting to create a confusing blur. The task of responding to sexual harassment and assault feels simultaneously more urgent and more daunting than ever.

Society is out of practice at this task; the same culture of silence that protected harassers also suppressed the public response to their crimes. Many people struggle even to know which questions to ask, and worry that if they ask the wrong ones, they might become part of the problem.

There is a temptation to simplify matters by viewing all harassers and their offenses as equally awful, or, alternatively, as equally misunderstood. But to be fair and effective, any system needs to make distinctions: to sort Harvey Weinstein from Roy Moore; and Louis C.K. and Matt Lauer from Al Franken.

The legal system, while quite different from the court of public opinion, offers principles and reasoning that we can use to evaluate each case as it flares.

SLIPPERY SLOPES AND CONSEQUENCES

Until recently, all of those accused, no matter the severity of their offenses, faced the same consequences: generally none. Protected by their power and authority, they kept their careers and reputations intact.

As that begins to change, some worry that we might bungle the job. "Taking harassment seriously also requires making serious distinctions," Jonah Goldberg, a conservative columnist, wrote recently for The Los Angeles Times. "And yet Franken's name is routinely listed alongside Moore's and Weinstein's."

Masha Gessen, writing in The New Yorker, worried we may be on the verge of a "sex panic."

Jane Curtin, a comedian who is a friend and former colleague of Mr. Franken's, compared the current atmosphere to McCarthyism. "It's just like the red menace," she said in an interview with The Times. "You don't know who's going to be next."

Many of those accused have lost their jobs, but for the most part, they are not facing legal consequences. Yet principles borrowed from criminal law can help us analyze whether our response to their actions is just and fair.

Criminal punishment tends to rest on two broad principles: the seriousness of the wrongdoing, and the perpetrator's intent in committing the crime.

Viewed through that lens, the accusations against Mr. Weinstein, which include rape, and Mr. Moore, who is accused of molesting teenage girls, are clearer-cut cases for punishment than those against, say, Louis C.K., who masturbated in front of adult women but did not touch them.

It's also important that courts do not consider only the moment of the crime itself in determining punishment. Our system also punishes defendants who threaten witnesses or obstruct justice, as well as others who help them do so. Here again, the accusations against Mr. Weinstein are especially extreme. According to a report by Ronan Farrow in The New Yorker, he hired ex-Israeli intelligence agents to intimidate victims and journalists into silence.

Dana Min Goodman and Julia Wolov, two of the women who have accused Louis C.K. of misconduct, have said they stayed silent for years in part because of pressure from Dave Becky, Louis C.K.'s manager. Mr. Becky has denied threatening them. But the women have said they feared that speaking would bring retribution.

ACCOUNTABILITY FOR HARM

The question of punishment is merely one factor in considering these cases. The wave of accusations has also led to demands that society recognize and repair the harm of sexual misconduct.

Caroline Framke, a culture critic for Vox, called for an accounting of the "graveyard of potential cut short by careless cruelty."

The principles of civil law, which are intended to make victims whole and ensure that no one profits from wrongdoing, can offer useful guidance about what is fair, and what is necessary.

A central principle is that the person at fault, not the victim, should bear the cost of the harms of wrongdoing. In law school, budding attorneys learn the "eggshell plaintiff" rule, which says that defendants are responsible for all of the harm they cause, even if the injuries were made more extreme because, say, the victim's skull was as thin as an eggshell. Otherwise, the reasoning goes, the costs will fall on the victims — a more unfair outcome than holding perpetrators responsible for unexpectedly severe damages.

It is now becoming clear that there is not a one-to-one correlation between the objective egregiousness of sexual misconduct and the damage it can cause.

Louis C.K.'s actions may have been less extreme than Mr. Weinstein's. But Ms. Goodman and Ms. Wolov have said they felt they could no longer work on projects involving him or his manager — a category that grew to include a large chunk of the comedy industry as Louis C.K.'s career took off.

And the Emmy-award-winning writer Kater Gordon told The Information that when Matthew Weiner, her boss on the show "Mad Men," told her that he "deserved to see her naked," he undermined her confidence and ambition. (Mr. Weiner has said that he does not remember making that comment, and would not speak that way to a colleague.)

Held up next to the allegations against Mr. Weinstein or Mr. Moore, those words may seem like a misdemeanor. But the harm was nevertheless severe, Ms. Gordon says, because she left the television industry, abandoning a promising career.

Women are often told to grow a "thicker skin" and become less sensitive to harassment. But the eggshell plaintiff rule suggests a different conclusion: that the harassers should bear the costs of the harm they impose, even on "thin-skinned" victims.

We must also consider harms that go beyond the immediate victims. Less diverse workplaces offer women fewer opportunities to find mentorship and achieve success; research suggests such workplaces are also less profitable.

Holding particular harassers responsible for harms suffered by an entire industry or gender is difficult; there are too many contributing factors for it to be easy to apportion blame. Collective harm may be more suited to government- or society-level responses. But again, the harm is there. The question is who ought to bear the cost.

WHY IT'S HARD TO THINK THROUGH THESE ACCUSATIONS

As more men are tarred as bad actors, and once-cherished public figures become pariahs, imposing responsibility can feel uncomfortable, even alarming.

People worry that we are sliding down a slippery slope to neo-puritanism, or in the throes of a witch hunt for sexual impropriety. Perhaps it will turn out that we are. But social science research suggests that this discomfort is a natural consequence of shifting social norms, not necessarily a sign that the changes are going too far.

Humans are wired to conform to group judgments. Dan Kahan, a professor at Yale Law School, argued in an influential paper that we rely more on our peers' opinions than on actual laws to determine what behavior is right or wrong.

In the famous "conformity study" by the researcher Solomon Asch, a majority of participants chose to select a clearly incorrect answer to a question rather than defy the group and cease being a peer in good standing.

Partisanship was a crucial element in the issue of sexual assault during the 2016 presidential campaign, when Donald J. Trump was heard on tape boasting about grabbing women's genitals. The ensuing public debate led many women to discuss their experiences for the first time.

That was a shift away from the previous rules, in which victims stayed silent. But the partisan aspect of the episode meant that the new conversation about assault was still a form of group morality and a way to conform to group judgments. Opposing sexual assault became a way to call Mr. Trump unfit for office, and so it fit within the familiar context of partisan rivalry.

But the more recent accusations — affecting Democrats as well as Republicans — have scrambled that partisan logic and made such group moral decision-making more difficult.

Meanwhile, the old norms of gender roles and hierarchies have not disappeared, and may conflict with new demands for accountability. There is no safe harbor of conformity to be had.

It would be convenient if doing the right thing were easy. But bringing long-hidden harms to the surface cannot help disturbing the status quo. Accounting for years of wrongdoing is costly, and dismantling hierarchies that fostered harm can lead, in the short term, to chaos. Now society must decide how many of those costs it is willing to bear.

CHAPTER 2

In the Home

There was a time when it was assumed — by men and women — that a woman's primary role was homemaker. And for a long time, that made sense. However, the rise of the machine age during the early 20th century turned homemakers from producers into consumers. Women could now buy products that helped to reduce the physical labor required to run a household and care for a family. By the 1930s, women were presented with more options for how to spend their time than ever before. More women began to work outside the home, and the role of home-maker became devalued.

A Woman's Opinion

LETTER | **BY THE NEW YORK TIMES** | **OCT. 13, 1989**

TO THE EDITOR OF THE NEW YORK TIMES:

I have been much interested in the reduction in the price of The New York Times and the comments of prominent men upon this change, but have not yet seen the opinion of any woman reader printed. The motto of your paper, "All the News That's Fit to Print," certainly makes it a favorite as a woman's paper. Now that we have the "new" woman, who has and expresses an opinion upon every subject — though I am not in sympathy with that movement and took pleasure in signing a pro-test against it, feeling that the "affairs of the Nation" are safer in the hands of my husband and other good men, and that woman's work lies in the home and its far-reaching influences — I do occasionally wish to express an opinion publicly, and the reduction in the price of The New

York Times, which paper has been an important part of our daily home life for six years, I feel sure meets with the hearty approval and appreciation of its many women readers. This brings a paper of the highest class within the easy reach of the refined woman in moderate circumstances. In my humble opinion, there is no other newspaper to compare with it, and I personally feel it is cheap at any price.

A HOMEMAKER WHO READS THE NEW YORK TIMES EVERY DAY, NEW YORK.

Shall Wives Be Wage Earners?

BY THE NEW YORK TIMES | SEPT. 24, 1906

DR. SIMON N. PATTEN, who occupies the Chair of Political Economy in the University of Pennsylvania and has written many books on economics, says in The Independent of Sept. 20 that brides whose husbands earn less than, say, twenty dollars a week ought to work in the factory, or in the shop or office, according to previous training, to help out the family expenses. Wives used to do a great deal of household work that specialized labor has taken from them, such as weaving, butter-making, and the like, therefore modern husbands must find them harder to support. The wife's work as a homemaker, too, has fallen in estimation:

> As agencies outside her home begin to do her work better than she can, her methods, in the natural course of events, become obsolete, and she struggles for her successes with tools which command less respect from her group than they did when their use impressed husband and children with her competence and mastery of resource.

He speaks sympathetically of the situation of the wife imbued with the old spirit of "service-altruism" — that is, of exercising an influence for good over husband and children through performance by her own hands of "the unsalaried functions of cook, laundress, and dressmaker." "Income-altruism," the contribution from some gainful occupation to her husband's salary, is her true way of salvation:

> Her affairs are frequently complicated further by her husband, who is likely to belong to the class that pours forth enormous numbers of half-equipped, half-energized men. Her typical mate is of the economic rank between those of the day laborer and the business man of initiative and independent movement — the grade recruited with clerks, stenographers, and salesmen — indifferently trained, perfunctory people, absent-mindedly following routine ways. Task for task, they are inferior to their wives, for they do not steadily care to maintain high traditions, to gauge themselves at the last notch of their engine. They are slovenly

when neatness would increase their value, and wastefully careless in exe-cution when precision would follow concentration of thought. Industrial shiftlessness condemns the wife to a hopeless round of harder work than the man will ever do.

For the benefit of these wives, and especially for such as would be freed from a cramped tenement-house existence, Dr. Patten would have enacted a special National labor law. He would have the factory transformed for woman's convenience, "the factory regarded as a public utility and regulated for the general welfare as the streets are cleaned for the city's healthfulness"; he would supervise the areas of production, and "Federalize them if need be, to bulwark the citizens of an industrial republic"; and he predicts that "radical provisions will undoubtedly be necessary to safeguard the hard-won rights of the swelling numbers of women in the factories."

All of which, we think, lacks pertinence. If the old household labors of woman on the agricultural plane have disappeared through the specialization of industries, she and society should be the gainers. The increment of the specialized economy is clearly hers in the form of a larger leisure, or, at least, of less drudgery than fell to the lot of her grandmother. It arises primarily, and inevitably, in the increased earning power and opportunities of the husband under improved mod-ern conditions. But if he be a lout and improvident, without ambition to increase a small salary, that fact furnishes the very best reason why society and the Federal Government should not be revolutionized to provide and protect occupations which the bride could follow only pre-cariously at best. Dr. Patten's scheme would make a sort of Socialistic provision for the maintenance in wedlock of vast numbers of his "half-equipped, half-energized men" at the expense of womanhood and of motherhood. If women choose to marry men of this type we cannot believe that it is the duty of the Government to strive to make it eco-nomically possible.

Woman's Place The Home.

LETTER | BY THE NEW YORK TIMES | APRIL 29, 1904

The wife has more important duties than increasing the family income.

TO THE EDITOR OF THE NEW YORK TIMES:

Prof. Patten's opinion as to the duty of a wife whose husband earns less than $20 per week betrays an utter unconsciousness of the result of such an attempt to increase the family income. If a couple begin their married life by assuming their own duties — the husband that of wage-earner, the wife that of homemaker — the ideal of the home is preserved, even though misfortune may make it afterward necessary that this ideal be set aside for a time. But if an able-bodied man consents at any time for his wife to help in furnishing the support for the family he continues to be willing and finally becomes even anxious that her efforts in that direction should increase, allowing his own to decrease in proportion.

But the greatest harm is done to the children of such a family. When the mother's attention is turned toward winning a support for these children she cannot make a home for them, however much she may wish to do so. The house becomes to them merely a place where an occasional meal may be had at a time convenient for them, and where they may sleep whenever the streets fail to hold their interest. Heredity, environment, intemperance, bad company, all together, are not so powerful in producing criminals as that lack of home influences which turns loose on the world a swarm of untrained, undisciplined, characterless young men and women already old in a knowledge of evil. It is utterly impossible that any kind of a home can exist without the constant oversight of the wife and mother.

ABBA WOODWORTH, ORANGE, N. J.

Women's Place: Home or Office

BY EUNICE FULLER BARNARD | AUG. 10, 1930

Mrs. Thomas A. Edison and Mrs. Franklin D. Roosevelt discuss the satisfactions of careers inside the home and outside it, now that invention has changed all the old ways of life.

WOMEN'S LIFE, perhaps more than men's, has been transformed by the machine age. Men, to be sure, in inventing the machines have changed the conditions of their own work as producers. But women, so far as their physical work in the home is concerned have, it is generally recognized, been turned from producers into consumers.

What are women going to do about their institution of the home? Should they use their new-found leisure to become producers of new cultural values there? Or should they follow physical production into the outside world? Two answers to these questions are given, in what follows, by women peculiarly associated in differing capacities with the new age — Mrs. Thomas A. Edison, wife of the inventor, and Mrs. Franklin D. Roosevelt, wife of the Governor of New York, and herself a teacher.

WHEN MRS. EDISON, in a radio talk the other day, urged as a necessary basis of national stability, that women re-enter and re-dignify the profession of home-making, thousands of feminine listeners, in farm house, apartment and Summer hotel, heard her attentively. For here was a kind of indirect confirmation of what every woman knows or at least suspects — that by the side of the genius invariably stands some woman who not only looks after the mechanics of his life, but provides him with that sense of security and companionship that is the essence of the word "home." Moreover, here was a statement of woman's place in the machine age by the wife of one of that age's chief creators.

As a representative of the profession she advocates, Mrs. Edison has a unique claim to be heard. For forty-four years, as wife of the

BETTMAN/GETTY

Mrs. Thomas A. Edison (left) pictured with her husband and family in 1922. Mrs. Franklin D. Roosevelt (right) in 1928.

inventor, noted for his insatiable zest for work and his disregard of its conventional hours, she has kept the home fires burning evenly, serenely and with that magic glow known as charm.

Out in the gabled red brick house, set amid spreading lawns and flower beds in Llewellyn Park at West Orange, where she came in the 1880s as a bride, today as the wife of the world-renowned inventor, unmoved by the contemporary urge toward change and ostentation, she still carries on. In these same rooms, fragrant now with the memories of a long family life, the six Edison children grew up, and from here in later years have gone out those gracious influences for community betterment which have been Mrs. Edison's constant contribution to the life of her town.

Indeed, in the restful reaches of her time — mellowed drawing rooms, brightened now with Summer chintzes and bowls of flowers, heat and hurry and change itself seem shut out. Just beyond, a deep, oval conservatory with groups of wicker chairs embowered in greenery stretches its inviting length, and somewhere outside one knows that a cow is grazing gently on sunny lawns. Unobtrusively, in a corner beside a fireplace, an organ rears its gilded pipes as if ready at any moment to fill the air with measured, sonorous tones. In such a house as this, with its pleasant divans and arches and ample mirrors, Alice might have gone through the looking-glass that Summer day many years ago.

And in the centre of it, like the spirit of the house itself, is Mrs. Edison, a gracious figure, white-clad with subtle touches of rose and black. Her brown eyes under a broad brow that somehow reminds one of Mr. Edison's own, look forth with a lovely serenity that might well be the despair of many a younger woman.

It is no wonder, one feels, that, like the artist in any calling, she should believe that life is not long enough for the perfection of one's home-making technique and that no amount of talent and education and penetration is too great for devotion to it. While the machine age may have changed the conditions, far from driving women out of the home, she believes, it should give them new opportunities within it. With something of this sort in mind, doubtless, she said the other day that if the family ex-chequer is so limited one must choose between sending the girl or the boy to college, the girl should have the preference so that she may have for her future homemaking the broadened cultural point of view that should constitute woman's new contribution.

Mrs. Edison's plea is for the recognition and elevation of the home-making profession in the public mind, and for the revaluation of its opportunities in the new era. If woman will only grasp the vast new possibilities which the machine civilization has put into her hands, she can, Mrs. Edison believes, raise her own institution of the home to cultural heights before undreamed of. She can play a major part in developing in America a general artistic appreciation. It may be her peculiar privilege to raise our cultural level to a par with our industrial achievement. As a bar to this, Mrs. Edison sees only woman's mistaken idea that she, too, must enter the economic world.

"Women today with their new leisure," she said, "have an opportunity such as they have never before possessed for their own cultural development and for a consequent enrichment of the home life. It seems incredible that they should throw away this finer opportunity for cultivating their minds and spend this time to earn money for new clothes to put upon their backs. Yet too often nowadays women are dissatisfied with what their husbands can provide. They seem to forget that our mothers under much harder circumstances got along without money. Where they had to preserve and bake and sometimes weave and make their own clothes, we have machinery to make all these tasks easy, or to take them out of the home entirely.

"Today for the first time the woman in the home can continue to develop her individual talents. Whether in art, in languages, in writing or music, she can enrich her own and her children's skill and appreciation. Even the woman in moderate circumstances today can make a beautiful setting for the family life such as was only possible for the woman of great wealth in former generations. Labor-saving devices have given her the time to read and study and go to lectures and concerts. Indeed, in this way it sometimes seems as if she had an undue advantage over the man in the modern world. She may systematically take the children to the art museums until perhaps she may create an atmosphere where art, as in Italy, is a part of life. She may develop the musical life of the home, making it center perhaps about a family orchestra, with each child playing a different instrument. Here again, as in Italy, and with the new aid of the radio, operas and symphonies may be popularly studied and known. Instead of being satisfied as now to hear them once, we might be really versed in them, making them part of ourselves."

IF WE ARE EVER to stop our habit of artistic "dipping," Mrs. Edison believes that it must be through a revaluation of art in the home. There, so to speak, in the cultural nursery of the nation, should be laid in the new mechanical age the foundations of an art-appreciation as deep as that of the Italians and of an ideal of thorough knowledge as stable as that of the Germans.

Even the mother who works outside the home to earn greater educational opportunities for her children should weigh well, Mrs. Edison believes, the advantages of which she is depriving them in the shape of her watchful solicitude, which must, from the nature of the relation, be greater than that of any outside person. The nurse or the neighbor to whom she may turn over the children may keep them physically safe, but she can rarely inculcate the spiritual serenity which is the highest contribution of the right kind of mother.

WHILE EVERY WOMAN as well as every man, in Mrs. Edison's opinion, should have some trade to which she can turn in case of need, she doubts whether — even before marriage — the college girl who is not under the necessity of repaying her parents for her education should turn to an outside occupation. Her greater contribution, Mrs. Edison thinks, can be made by enriching the home life of her father and mother and brothers and sisters, and through community work. As for the young husband and wife without children, both working in shops or offices and eating about in restaurants, they, too, she thinks, are missing the deeper values of the home as a place of refuge, quiet and spiritual growth.

"Both the man and the woman," she said, "should regard the wife's position of home executive as for her the finest possible career. In my opinion, women are just as intelligent as men, but they should recognize that they can use their intelligence to best advantage in making the home attractive instead of in meeting the hardships of a man's world, where he has the start of long years of experience.

"One thing that has driven women into business and the professions," she said, "is the fact that man has not appreciated her contribution in the home. He has not taken her task on a par with his. Often, the better home-maker she is, the more perfect and inviting she has made the home, the less he values her achievement, because he does not see the evidences of the labor and the planning that have gone into this result. So she turns to an outside field where her work is recognized.

"Another thing that oftentimes has irked the woman in the home has been her questionable economic status. She has been deeply humiliated by having to ask for every quarter and dime. If woman is to remain the home-maker, she must be given the same measure of dignity and financial independence that she has in working outside. After the man's business need, the savings account and the allowances for running the house and for the children's expenses have been taken care of in the family budget, the remainder should be equally divided between husband and wife as the personal income of each. Then the money question, the cause of so much unpleasantness, is out of sight altogether. As to the household bills, the wife, if that is desirable, should be perfectly capable of attending to them out of the budget without bothering her husband about them.

"On the technical side, of course, the woman should see to it that the home is run with the same businesslike dispatch as is the man's office. Everything should be organized and departmentalized.

"The whole system of household service should be on a sounder actual and psychological basis. The terminology should be changed. Household helpers should not be referred to as servants or domestics or as hired help, but as home assistants skilled in various departments. Cooking, for instance, might well be looked upon as a more highly skilled occupation than filing. There should be training schools for such home assistants where they could learn how to perform the various household tasks in the most efficient manner and from which they could graduate to command wages in accordance with their efficiency. The assistant could not then, as often now under the present agency system, be recommended for a job she has no ability to fill, any more than a man with no experience could be placed in a factory at running a lathe, and we should not have the present spectacle of a cook earning $80 and cooking no better than when she was getting $40. The relatively unskilled person would expect to take a minor position and receive less money, winning promotion, as he or she increased in competence.

"Of course, this implies that the home executive, too, should be educated for her calling. She should no more be in the position of assigning tasks which she does not understand than should the foreman of a factory. From the beginning the whole undercurrent of a girl's training should be for the household in its new and enlarged sense. First at home, then at school, and finally in college she should be taught the technique of her profession. She should be instructed not only in its processes of cooking and child care and its physical materials and machines, but especially in the cultural and spiritual side of home-making.

"The colleges must adapt themselves to woman's need. They must work out a course for the girl different from that for the boy, so that she may major in the cultural subjects with practical home-making requirements. Her curriculum, for instance, might emphasize comprehensive background courses in history, science, music and art appreciation with special attention to the use of English, spoken and written. Only with some such program as this, I believe, can the home attain its true spiritual function in the machine age."

WHETHER IT IS woman's new mission to be the guardian and upbuilder of the national culture through the home, Mrs. Roosevelt was not sure. Herself a product of the new age, the mother of five children, teacher and vice principal in a New York girls' school, manager of a furniture-making enterprise on her Hyde Park estate, worker on political and civic committees, hostess at the Executive Mansion in Albany, she is simultaneously a homemaker. Indeed, if numbers have any bearing, she should be given a special place at the top of the record, for she is the active executive of three households, the official home in Albany, the Roosevelt country place at Hyde Park and the town house in Sixty-fifth Street.

Already a grandmother, she has the bearing and the interests of a woman in her twenties. Commuting day after day from Albany to New York to be at her schoolroom in the East Eighties at a quarter of nine o'clock in the morning and back again to preside at tea in the Executive Mansion in the late afternoon, seems only to have intensified her infectious vitality. Indeed, like her uncle, Theodore Roosevelt, she seems not so much to have grasped at modern opportunities as to have made them the unobtrusive servants of her own genius and personality.

Buoyant as a college girl even at half-past eight of a stuffy Summer morning in town, between two speaking engagements up-State, she seemed a peculiarly fitting spokesman for woman in the new civilization that machines have made. On the walls of her well-ordered drawing room old prints of sea scenes intrigued the eye, a witness to her husband's hobby. Somewhere in the background a butler methodically answered an insistent succession of telephone calls.

"Home," she said, "is never a place, but an atmosphere. In our growingly complex life, the way a woman creates this must be largely an individual matter governed by the conditions in which she is placed. As long as she has little children, if she is not obliged to contribute money to the home, I should feel as does Mrs. Edison, that all other work or indeed play, of her own, should be adjusted so as not to interfere with their best care.

"With all the scientific aids of modern times there still are certain things which the mother can do personally for her children that even a good nurse or governess usually cannot do. Just being at home with them at lunch and in the afternoon when they come from school is a duty she ought to lay upon herself unless it is economically necessary for her to be away, it should be her pleasure always to be there when they come in asking for her.

"When the question of children does not enter in, when they have grown up and gone away to school or college or homes of their own and the husband still has his outside work and interests, then it seems to me that woman's work outside the home becomes almost entirely an individual problem. What would be right for one woman might not be right for another. Some women are not strong enough for any occupation in addition to home-making. Fortunately it seems to be true that those who really want to do something else — doubtless due to the buoyancy that gives them the desire — have the physical strength to accomplish it.

"And for many women, I believe that the happy spirit and enlarged interests gained through the outlet for their capacities in outside work makes for a better home atmosphere than would otherwise be the case. In the modern day of apartments designed to take up as little time as possible, the woman who sits at home is apt to be idle and not very contented. It is quite true that every forward looking woman wants to go on educating herself all her life through. But one cannot always study. Often more education is to be gained in other ways. Particularly in the artistic field the machine age has made continued amateur study increasingly difficult. Only the few — men and women — have artistic talents, and those they possess are being less and less developed because of mechanical devices. Now, for instance, at a turn of the dial, the home can have better music than mother used to make.

"For a person with talents in more practical lines there is no longer sufficient work to do in the home. Today women who do canning and baking and washing are very largely employed in the big commercial canneries, bakeries and laundries. In my lifetime I have seen this revolution in women's work — the older age of individualistic production in the home giving way to mass production. We must face the new homes we have, in which there are almost no essential tasks for the daughter of the house.

"Moreover, whatever our preferences in the matter, the fact remains that the present age with its wholesale methods is forcing women out of the home as a mere matter of their own economic survival. Few of us see any loss of prestige to women in the process. It was different fifty years ago. Back in Margaret Fuller's day, for instance, when every mild innovation in woman's customary home-keeping routine was fought with a bitterness that now seems almost incredible.

"Nor do I believe that women's natures necessarily become harsher from meeting the outside world. In my opinion there are quite as many obstacles to be overcome in running a household as in any extraneous occupation. Indeed, home problems usually are so personal in nature and workers in the home live under such close conditions of day-in-and-day-out association, that sometimes the difficulties occasion more emotional strain than would any outside work.

"It is true, doubtless, that women have not attained the same standing in the general occupational field that men have, but that is because they are still in the minority. Relatively to their numbers, they have done well. When a woman puts her whole self into her work, there are few heights to which she cannot attain.

"One of the most serious features of the taking of work out of the family life, as machines have largely done, is not in the effect on the mother, but on the children and young people of the household. To-day, under modern conditions of city life, with no wood to chop and bring in, no clothes to be made and little necessary cooking to be done, the old-fashioned 'chores' that the children did nave largely disappeared. The family is not an economic unit, in the old sense. Parental authority has weakened. The hard conditions of life in other days reinforced it. For it was then obvious to the child that bringing in the wood and picking berries were necessities, if the family was to keep warm or be fed.

"Today, in short, for both the young woman and the young man physical surroundings no longer give them the discipline of common tasks which once created the family solidarity, and we have not yet discovered any substitute. Hurried and mastered by machines, neither women nor men have stopped to find out what they ultimately want. Too often we are servants of the machine, drifting with the spirit of the age. We have got to get back to the idea that along with the mastery of nature, we must develop spiritually, as Mrs. Edison has suggested. We must have a religion, and by this I mean that we must find some reason that makes it worth while to develop the best that is in us. Then we shall have the spirit of the home under any conditions. The art of home-making has changed with the new age, but whether the woman must work in or out of the home, that spirit need not decline."

Where Is Women's Place?

REVIEW | BY BEVERLY GRUNWALD | AUG. 9, 1964

'After Nora Slammed the Door: American Women in the 1960s — The
Unfinished Revolution' by Eve Merriam. Published in 1964 by The World
Publishing Company.

WHAT REALLY HAPPENED when Nora slammed the door? According to
Eve Merriam, poet, television writer and author of numerous books for
children, she never left her doll house — and, as a consequence, American women today remain unfulfilled. The happy housewife pictured in
advertisements is a myth. The "Woman's Revolution" is a century old,
but emancipation is still a battle and woman is still a second-class citi-
zen. Mrs. Merriam is as worried as Simone de Beauvoir in the "Second
Sex" and as vociferous as Betty Friedan in "The Feminine Mystique."
But she is not so clinical.

More than half of the nation's wives are housewives. To be just a
housewife, Mrs. Merriam thinks, is to assume a loathesome, inferior
role. It is unfulfilling and stultifying. Middle-class women, particularly
those with a college education, must do more with their lives than keep
house and tend husband and babies. A woman must earn money or else
she will be forever dependent and subservient to her husband. She cannot respect herself without a bank balance of her own. She must find a
job — and not just any old job will do. She must enter the professions and
aim for the top, even though the top is tough for the career woman who
makes it. Men don't like her; women voice the phrase "career woman"
as an epithet. It's almost as bad as being "just a housewife."

The women who live alone (four million of them), whether unmar-
ried, divorced or widowed, also come up for scrutiny. In a togetherness-
prone society, they are natural suspects. Why aren't they married?
Can they be trusted? What about their odd female friends? In a poetic
stanza (and there are several interspersed with the earnest prose) the
author laments:

*The women with empty wedding
rings in their eyes
walk into the married room
And I pity them.*

For that matter, Eve Merriam pities most of her sex. She cannot abide the "total housewife." ("Staying home full-time forever is no longer a fit occupation for a full-grown woman.") We are told that the total housewife smokes more, has more extramarital affairs, develops ulcers and other ailments. (Housemaid's knee?) There is a greater incidence of juvenile delinquency where Mother is in constant residence. The author realizes that there aren't enough jobs for *all* women who want to work, but she sees this as no excuse for selling the housewife on her non-job or making her the patsy for 57 varieties of lotion and countless detergents. The "consuming" housewife passages are the author's funniest and most ironic.

Mrs. Merriam has strong opinions not every reader will savor. Despite the reformers, it is still a fact that many women are happy and fulfilled in being "just housewives." (It's books like these that stir up guilt feelings.) If they are intelligent and sufficiently propelled, they need not stagnate. There are jobs to be done and projects to be undertaken at home or part time outside. It is not how much one makes but what one makes of oneself that counts. Surely, Mrs. Merriam, money isn't everything. And what about love? You never mention it. Happy marriages do exist, you know.

What lies ahead for the Noras? A good part of the author's housewife thesis has been developed before, but few proposed solutions have been as resourceful. City, state and Federal Government agencies, she feels, must get into the act to save apathetic womanhood. There must be communes — new apartment projects wherein families would live together. Bring back grandma, the spinster aunt, retired uncle: in true cooperative spirit, all would donate their services for housework, baby sitting, cooking, hobbies, maintenance, in a community pool to be shared by other families. A rather drastic arrangement for finding your identity — but it might lift a burden from the psychiatrist.

Men and Housework: Do They or Don't They?

BY NADINE BROZAN | NOV. 1, 1980

THE AMERICAN HUSBAND is willingly pitching in to do domestic chores at home, so that his wife can more easily be employed outside the home.

The American husband is doing dishes and folding laundry grudgingly, even though his wife's work may augment his income.

The American husband may say he helps out at home, but save for tending the lawn and taking out the garbage, he's not contributing much.

Contradictory though they may seem, all those findings are encompassed in studies conducted by four advertising agencies on how men view the changing role of women and how they are affected in their personal lives by those changes. The agencies were: Cunningham & Walsh; Benton & Bowles; Doyle Dane Bernbach; Batten, Barten, Durstine & Osborne.

The interest is more than coincidental, agency executives agreed. As a spokesman for Cunningham & Walsh, which has issued two reports on the topic, the newest one this week, put it: "Three years ago everyone was interested in the working woman; she represented such a huge market. Now agencies are realizing that the lives of husbands had to change, too. Ads for beer have always been telecast during ballgames, maybe we should be showing soap flake commercials during those times.

Apart from differences among the studies in the focus of questions and statistical methodology, differences in responses depended largely on the way men viewed the role of women as a whole. Three of the four agencies categorized their respondents into groups based on those views: Benton & Bowles, for example, called them "Progressives," "Traditionalists," "Ambivalents" and "All Talk, No Action."

Telephone responses from 200 men in 20 cities who were interviewed last year, led the authors of the B.B.D.O. report, "Men's Image of Today's Women," to the conclusion that "Today's man wants his woman to work at two jobs — one outside the home and one inside the home. Men may be sympathetic to the fact that this is a tough juggling act for any woman. Yet the majority are not willing to lift the traditional household responsibilities from their wives. The indications are that men would rather pay for labor-saving devices for their wives than labor at the wifely tasks themselves."

A GOOD MOTHER

Eighty percent of those men said that the quality they most wanted in their wife was that she be a good mother and, although they approved of employment of women, they still expected her to assume responsibility for household chores, shopping and child-rearing. More than 75 percent said their wives were primarily responsible for cooking, 78 percent considered cleaning the bathroom her domain. Of all chores, the one that men seemed most unlikely to do was the laundry.

By contrast, the Benton & Bowles study, entitled "American Consensus: Men's Changing Role in the Family of the 80's," called men "unexpectedly fair-minded about acknowledging their responsibilities in helping out with the housework." The report continued: "And they're not just paying lip service to this responsibility. They are doing many household chores in quite significant numbers. The chores they report doing range from the more expected dishwashing and taking out the garbage to such non-traditional chores as shopping for food, cooking for the family, doing the laundry, cleaning the bathroom and taking care of the children."

No matter who was doing the research, the men reported on seemed to be taking on their tasks with considerable ambivalence. As a result, in the Benton & Bowles survey by mail of 452 men, six of every 10 agreed that "the family is stronger if husband and wife share responsibilities, including providing income for the family." But 70 percent also agreed that "unless it is an economic necessity, a family is better off if the woman of the house does not work."

'EQUAL RESPONSIBILITY'

Eighty-eight percent of the men in that study said that the husband should at least "help out" with chores if the wife was employed, and 54 percent said they felt that domestic chores ought to be the "equal responsibility of the husband and wife." If the wife is not employed, 53 percent felt the husband should help.

In a given two week period, 80 percent of all the men said they had taken care of children in households with children under 12 years old and 47 percent had helped cook a meal; 39 percent had vacuumed the house, 33 percent had cooked an entire meal, 32 percent had done the food shopping and 29 percent the laundry.

But age, in this study as in the others, was sometimes indicative of a man's attitudes toward chores. For example, in the Benton & Bowles research, the "progressives," half of whom were under 35 years old, did more than any other category: 90 percent of them washed dishes and 80 percent did vacuuming. But the "All Talk, No Action" segment, also largely under 35, who said they accepted many egalitarian principles, performed fewer chores than any group save the generally older "traditionalists."

According to their answers, the 300 men from 20 cities and suburbs telephoned last November by Doyle Dane Bernbach seemed more resistant to household work, even though they had specifically approved of women becoming brain surgeons.

Barbara Michael, a vice president and group research director for the agency, wrote in the report, "The major disadvantage that the typical husband perceives in having a working wife is the effect not upon the children but upon himself: a husband has to spend more time on household chores that he doesn't like. And with the exception of lawns and home repair, he pretty much doesn't like any of them." The fear of detrimental effects on children was followed in depth of concern by fear of a decline in cleanliness standards and a sense that the extra income was not sufficient compensation for inconvenience.

As Miss Michael wrote, "Always keep in mind the male dragon in the kitchen is a reluctant one."

TAKING OUT THE GARBAGE

Similarly, the two studies done by Cunningham & Walsh, encompassing 1,000 married men and emphasizing the male role in grocery shopping and cooking, said: "When not cooking, some husbands are helping around the house in other ways. Taking out the garbage is the man's primary household assignment. Almost half vacuum most or some of the time and two out of five wash the dishes. One in three makes beds and loads the washing machine, while one in four cleans the bathroom, dusts and dries dishes. Husbands leave the cleaning of the refrigerator and the oven to their mates."

"The picture that emerges," the report continues, "is that a sizable minority of husbands throughout the country are taking more responsibility around the house. For the majority however, the apron strings have not been tied behind their backs. The working status of women has not had a thunderous impact on their husbands' traditional role at home."

Still, the prognosis is not all bleak. "We predict," the authors of the report stressed, "that what is now a small nucleus of homemaking husbands will grow into a significant segment, demanding the attention of marketers. More and more the American husband will be wondering as he moves through the supermarket aisles, 'What shall I serve for dinner tonight?' "

Women Who Mean Business

BY NANCY RUBIN | OCT. 12, 1980

THEY COME FROM every area of life, from every age group, but their goals are the same: to turn the home environment into a profitable business venture.

Some, such as Laura Horowitz, president of Editorial Experts Inc. of Alexandria, Va., have succeeded beyond their wildest expectations, translating their talents into million-dollar ventures. Others, such as Babette Feibel, owner of Abel Creations Company, a Columbus, Ohio, maker of custom toys, draw a moderate living from their home enterprises. And many, including Dora Back of After Six Secretarial Services of Fords, N.J., regard their home businesses as secondary income, something to fall back on in case of sudden unemployment or impending retirement.

They are women who own home-based businesses, and they are part of a new national trend that has seen women establish businesses five times as rapidly as men within the last decade.

The most recent figures of the Federal Bureau of Labor Statistics indicate that there were 1.9 million self-employed women in 1979, representing a 43 percent increase in women's entrepreneurship since 1972. Census Bureau figures, which are based on business tax returns and do not include women with large corporations, revealed a similar surge in women's enterprise since 1972 — 702,000 businesses owned by women in 1977, with receipts of $41.5 billion, representing a 30 percent increase in such concerns and a 72 percent increase in receipts.

According to the Census Bureau, almost half the businesses in the country that are owned by women are conducted from the home. The reasons behind their steady growth have been attributed to a variety of causes — higher education, an inflationary economy, child-care difficulties and dissatisfaction with the corporate establishment.

According to some economists, such as Michael Wachter, a professor at the University of Pennsylvania, the increase in women's entrepreneurship is a logical trend, one that he predicts will lead to a profound change during the decade. "One of the biggest institutional changes in the work force of the 1980's will be a growing accommodation of women, especially those with children," Dr. Wachter said. "And women working from their homes will be one major way to make that accommodation."

Beatrice Fitzpatrick, chief executive officer of the American Women's Economic Development Corporation, a Manhattan educational training and counseling center for women entrepreneurs, contends that the trend signals a profound social phenomenon: "The service-oriented economy, woman's historical and social roles and her special talents are coming together to make this the beginning of an age of great women entrepreneurs. Women have enormous ingenuity but not much capital, so it's natural for many of them to begin enterprises at home."

Other business advisers, such as Adele Kaplan, a manager at the Rutgers University Small Business Development Center, in Newark, believes that the increased number of female entrepreneurs is related to disillusionment with corporate opportunities. "Let's face it, many women in the corporate world aren't doing well, and all too often the myth exceeds the reality," Miss Kaplan said. "Women with managerial skills and stamina are beginning to realize they can turn those characteristics to better advantage as entrepreneurs."

Intrigued with the possibilities of the home-based business, Marion Behr, an Edison, N. J., freelance artist, and Wendy Lazar of Norwood, N. J., a broadcast journalist and author, founded the National Alliance of Home-Based Businesswomen and are conducting a national survey of women entrepreneurs. "Once women have education and work skills and find themselves at home with small children, starting a business is often a natural next step," said Mrs. Behr, who began the Women Working Home survey in 1978 and has contacts with home-based women entrepreneurs in 20 states. "For women who don't want the rat race of commuting and still want a career, it can be the best of all possible worlds."

Mrs. Behr and Mrs. Lazar have found there are more than 80 occupations and businesses being conducted from the home, including artists, lawyers, physicians, importers, detectives, media consultants, horticulturists, party planners and clothing manufacturers. "There's obviously a great need out there," Mrs. Behr said, "but we're dealing with an invisible work force, one nobody has ever paid attention to before."

The National Alliance of Home-Based Business Women is planning a book on its findings. Expected to appear next year, it will include a directory of 400 home businesswomen as well as articles. "Our goal is to create a business information network and to increase the visibility and status of these women," Mrs. Behr said.

One of the most serious problems of the home-based business is its amateur image, one that has been linked with the informal atmosphere of the 18th-century cottage industry. "The comment we keep seeing over and over on the questionnaire is, 'I'm treated like a hobbyist, and I resent that tremendously,' " observed Mrs. Behr. "We'd like to help women change that image."

Even successful home-based entrepreneurs concede that a residential location can be a formidable stumbling block. Laura Horowitz, whose million-dollar Editorial Experts Inc. depends on the employment of several hundred freelancers working from their homes and who herself works from hers in Alexandria, Va., acknowledges that self-discipline can be difficult.

Other home-based businesswomen, such as Cindy Lowe of Rainbow Squared Communications, operator of a Dallas editing firm, have observed that neighbors and their children can be troublesome: "When I first started the business some neighbors complained I no longer had time for them, and yet they still sent their children over to play," said Mrs. Lowe, who has a 3-year-old son.

Another frequently cited problem is the addition of extra staff, phones and equipment, and the gradual encroachment of a growing enterprise on the family's private life. Susan Gentry, who runs Talk of the Town, a $250,000-a-year party-planning service, from her San Francisco apartment and has just rented additional office space next door, commented, "While it's great to be able to work on projects anytime day or night, the flip side is that it's always there and you can't ever escape."

Judith Kalina, president of Fable Soft Sculpture Inc., an enterprise specializing in mythological crafts and sewing kits, situated in her Shenorock, N.Y., home, described the effect of her rapidly expanding business upon the house and her family life as a "personal invasion."

"Now that the business has begun to grow so quickly," she said, "I'm feeling overwhelmed about how much space it requires." Mrs. Kalina's $80,000 business occupies the front porch, dining room, basement and garage of her Westchester County home. "There's a delicate line as to when it's ideal to be home and when it's time to move out," she said.

For other women, the advantages of the home location are indisputable, particularly if their work requires around-the-clock attention, or if household demands such as young children or elderly parents warrant a woman's presence in the home. One such woman is Sara Evestone, an artist and mother of five children, who maintains several studios in her home in Wayside, N.J., who said, "I've had several opportunities to rent space outside the home, but found with babies and little children it was always difficult to rely upon sitters and other forms of child care." She plans to build additional rooms in her home to accommodate a growing business. "As it turned out, I was always more productive when I could work at home. Now, even though my children are older, I'd never consider moving the business out."

Considering the Place of the Working Parent in the Kitchen

BY RACHEL L. SWARNS | NOV. 16, 2014

EVERY NOVEMBER, I close my eyes and conjure up memories of Thanksgivings past. I remember roasted turkeys and hams, homemade stuffing and cranberry sauce, collard greens and candied yams, pecan and pumpkin pies, and my joyful mother in the center of it all.

She carried that spirit into weekday meals, too, cooking Cornish hens and rice pilaf, or eggplant parmigiana and garlic bread, or Bahamian specialties like fried fish and plantains. Having a working mother who was happy in the kitchen seemed completely natural when I was in middle school on Staten Island. I never imagined that I would be any different.

But these days, I must confess, dinnertime sometimes fills me with dread. Don't get me wrong; I've cooked some wonderful holiday meals for my husband and our two boys. I have been creative — sometimes — during the workweek, too.

But I have also been that working parent who roasted turkey breasts for Thanksgiving (instead of the whole bird) and followed it with generous servings of supermarket pie. I have relied on babysitters whose culinary expertise tended toward fish sticks and chicken nuggets. And on particularly hectic nights, I have consoled myself after breaking open a box of Annie's macaroni and cheese. (At least it's organic!)

Maybe you know the feeling? The struggle to find the time, energy and money to regularly prepare fresh, healthy, home-cooked meals frames the working lives of many parents in New York City and beyond.

Last week, dozens of parents responded to my call for a conversation about the challenges of juggling hectic work schedules and family dinners. In recent months, the topic has become the subject of some debate as researchers from North Carolina State University have argued that efforts to promote home cooking — by government officials, celebrity chefs and food writers — may do more harm than good.

The sociologists, who conducted in-depth interviews with 150 mothers, understand that everyone wants Americans to live healthier lives. But they argued that the home-cooking message ignores the time pressures, financial constraints and feeding challenges faced by working parents, particularly in an unsettled economy when many people are working multiple jobs with long and unpredictable hours.

"Suggesting that we return to the kitchen en masse will do little more than increase the burden so many women already bear," the sociologists wrote.

The report struck a nerve. No surprise there. After all, it flies in the face of advice coming from Michelle Obama, the first lady; Michael Pollan, the food writer; officials at the United States Department of Agriculture; and researchers at Pennsylvania State University, who reported this year that children with parents who spend more time cooking choose healthier foods later in life.

Some parents are embracing that message, turning away from processed foods and fast foods.

Karen Roos, an environmental educator and mother of three, who grew up a few blocks from me on Staten Island and still lives there, did just that a couple of years ago. No more supermarket roasted chickens, no more chicken nuggets, no more McDonald's.

"It's not even a thought any more to consider eating that," said Ms. Roos, who cooks most nights.

Other parents are struggling. A study published last year showed that about 56 percent of American adults spend time cooking on a given day, down from about 63 percent in the 1960s. The percentage of women who cooked dropped sharply, to 68 percent from 92 percent in 1965, as more women joined the work force.

Kelly Ann Harris, a lawyer who lives in Maplewood, N.J., said she loved the idea of cooking regularly for her 6-year-old daughter, but simply could not find the time. "How the heck am I going to work full time, food shop, cook, do laundry, interact with my child and actually sleep?" she asked.

BRYAN THOMAS FOR THE NEW YORK TIMES

Kelly Ann Harris, a lawyer, with her daughter, Kate, at home in Maplewood, N.J.

If you're well off, maybe you can turn to household help or increasingly popular services like Blue Apron, which delivers fresh ingredients for specific recipes that are ready to be transformed into home-cooked meals.

But for many families, that's simply not an option.

"First lady Obama has a full staff to prepare her meals," said Lashauna Brown, a single mother in Harlem who works as a case manager for a nonprofit agency. "As long as my child is not starving or being neglected, who cares how he is fed."

This is not an easy subject. For some of us, it stirs up feelings of guilt and shame when we consider the gap between the parents we are and the parents we wish we could be.

I strive to cook more, just like my mother, who worked as a teacher, school administrator and superintendent. I also strive to be kinder to myself about my limitations. So on Thanksgiving Day, you'll find my family shuttling from my in-laws in the Bronx to the place where I feel most at home during this holiday season: at my parents' table, on Staten Island.

I won't be feeling guilty. Several months ago, my 7-year-old son brought home a card he had written for me in school that began, "I love my mom because she is such a good cooker."

Sometimes what we do just might be enough.

More Women Find Room for Babies and Advanced Degrees

BY TAMAR LEWIN | MAY 7, 2015

THE SHARE of highly educated women who are childless into their mid-40s has fallen significantly over the last two decades, according to a new Pew Research Center analysis of data from the Census Bureau.

The decline is steepest among women in their 40s who have an M.D. or Ph.D. Last year, 20 percent reported having no children, compared with 35 percent in 1994. Among those who have a master's degree or higher, 22 percent are childless, down from 30 percent in 1994.

Demographers said that as the ranks of female professionals have grown, so, too, has the sense that career and motherhood need not be mutually exclusive. While finding the right balance of work and family may not be easy, they say, it has become an everyday challenge, rather than an unusual strain.

And many women who delayed childbearing as they were building their careers often find themselves wanting a family as they near the end of their reproductive years.

"As more women entered the labor force and became professionals, a lot of them put off having children, said William Frey, a demographer at the Brookings Institution, who was not involved in the analysis. "But then they realize that there's a biological clock, and they start playing catch up as they understand the importance of family life, and know that it's something they want."

Gretchen Livingston, the Pew senior researcher who did the analysis, said that with so many women now earning advanced degrees, the profile of the group has probably altered.

"From where I stand, as someone with a Ph.D., I see that lots of people get Ph.D.s now, and they don't all go off to be research professors," she said. "Perhaps it's a different group now, less single-mindedly focused on their career."

Then, too, she said, highly educated women are more likely to be married now than 20 years ago — and married women are more likely to have babies. Advances in reproductive technology have also increased fertility among older women, especially educated ones who can afford expensive procedures like in vitro fertilization.

Dr. Livingston said she could be the "poster girl" for her own research. She is 46, with a Ph.D. and two children — "two is the new four" she said — whom she waited to have until her late 30s.

Although it is closing, there is still an education gap as it relates to fertility and family size, with highly educated women less likely to become mothers or have a large family than women with little education. Among mothers with an advanced degree, 23 percent have only one child, and only 8 percent have four or more.

But among mothers who did not complete high school, 13 percent have only one child, and 26 percent have four or more.

Over all — education aside — 15 percent of women ages 40 to 44 are childless, the lowest proportion in at least a decade. That proportion was even lower, about 10 percent, in the mid-1970s, when data on lifetime childlessness first became available, but rose quickly from 1986 to 2006.

Hispanic and Asian women between 40 and 44 are more likely than white or black women to have had children. Just 10 percent of Hispanic women ages 40 to 44 have had no children, compared with 17 percent of white women in that age range.

Generally, Americans are having smaller families than they used to, with only children on the rise, and families of four or more children dwindling.

In 1976, 36 percent of women in their early 40s had four or more children, compared with just 12 percent in 2014. And 18 percent of mothers in their 40s had just one child last year, compared with 10 percent in 1976.

At least for the time being, younger women are charting a different course, with fewer babies.

"Since the 1990s, birth rates among women under 30 have been declining, particularly during the recession, and the younger the women, the bigger the decline," Dr. Livingston said.

CHAPTER 3

At Work

Although the primary role for women was once considered to be homemaker, some women — by choice or by necessity — followed a less conventional path, instead working outside the home. From Civil War nurses to doctors specializing in women's health, from professional baseball players during World War II and New York City cabdrivers in the 1950s to combat soldiers and pilots, women have held every kind of job imaginable. The question today is far less often whether to work but rather which of the thousands of professions from which to choose.

The Women and the War.

BY THE NEW YORK TIMES | AUG. 3, 1862

ONE OF THE FEATURES of this civil war, which, it is to be hoped, will not escape the notice of the historian, is the part women have taken in it. Probably the greatest peculiarity of American society is the kind of equal sympathy which women have in all the earnest affairs of the men. Whatever folly our public declaimers may have uttered year after year on "Women's Rights," practically, the women of America have "rights and privileges" in all that man does, and feels, and possesses, through the best medium — her sympathy. During all the long contests of principle which preceded this war, and of which it was the legitimate fruit, it is not too much to say that the great body of the women of the Free States stood firmly on the side of liberty and justice. The women, far more than the men in the North, have always been, in feeling and instinct, opposed to the Southern "sacred institution." When the war broke out, though acting the true part of women in calming rather than irritating hot passions, their loyalty to the Government showed itself as even more fervent, if less noisy, than in most of the men. With silent zeal and eagerness, they sat themselves down to intense and constant labor in preparing what should soothe the fevered pulse of the poor sick soldier, or should bind up his wounds, or administer to his health, or relieve the monotony of his desolate life in the hospital. Everywhere throughout the land, in distant mountain vallies, in farm-houses, in city palaces, in the West and on the seaboard, the little circle of American women met to ply with nimble fingers the needle for the camp and the hospital. Not being able to risk their own lives, they seemed to feel that too much could not be done for the brave men who were risking all for their common and beloved country. The vast stores of articles, the innumerable boxes of lint, the bales of shirts, drawers and clothes of every kind, the rolls of bandages, the quantities of jellies, wines, cordials, and comforts of every description, which have been sent on to Washington to the Sanitary Commission, or to individual regiments by our women, surpass belief. Wherever a hospital happens to be established near a Northern or Western city, the bounties poured out on the sick soldiers by fair hands are beyond all computation, and the only trouble seems to be that the poor men receive too many good things rather than too few. Happy the wounded private soldier who is carried to a Northern hospital. The wealthiest and fairest of our ladies are only too glad to relieve his hours of suffering. And what if this be sometimes overdone, and, as in the much laughed-over instance of a poor private in our Park hospital, he be asked by fourteen different ladies in one morning, "if they could wipe his fevered brow." We may be sure that the above-mentioned private enjoyed it, and that these attentions of pretty and refined women are the payment which these brave fellows most of all value for their patriotic services. As we have no medals or crosses of honor, or titles, or ranks, for distinguished services, the flattering and kind attention of a grateful people takes their place. We need not speak of the noble and self-sacrificing deeds of our women as nurses and attendants on the sick at the seats of war — many of them leaving the highest positions and comforts to work in the hospital-ship, and to bind the wounds and wash the sores of our poor soldiers; others writing their last letters, or attending to the last messages of love at death; and doing all this, not merely to our own men but to enemies — to the rebel wounded as well. But even more than this, who can tell of that silent patriotism all over this country, which has, without a struggle or a sigh, offered up what the heart most valued for the country's sake. Widows have sent their only and long-cherished sons, sisters their brothers, wives their husbands, and maidens their betrothed. If still greater reverses are to come, we will know that there is no depth of calamity which they will not share, and if more brilliant victories, they will be with us to temper our hot revenge, and spread abroad peace and good will again.

Whenever American women are mentioned in connection with this war, the phenomenon of the amazing ferocity and bitterness of Southern women will occur to the mind, and we cannot but ask ourselves its cause.

We believe it but a corresponding part to what we have been describing at the North. The American woman shares all things with the man. If he is a rebel and a barbarian, she will be so, too. If he hates the flag, she will hate it also. If he drinks from Yankee skulls and plays tattoo with Northern *tibioe*, she will display barbarism in her own way — by weak insults, by bitter taunts, by spitting in the faces of those who, as gentlemen, cannot protect themselves, by vulgar gestures and coarse abuse of the suffering. And inasmuch as in sympathy with the man's ferocity she has violated her own nature, so will she be ten times as much of a devil as he.

The Question of Lady Doctors.

LETTERS | BY THE NEW YORK TIMES | JAN. 8, 1865

VIEWS OF A REGULAR PHYSICIAN.

To the Editor of the New-York Times:

The public discussion in the columns of The Times, in regard to the alleged maltreatment of the lady students attending Bellevue Hospital, and the merit of the movement toward thorough female medical education now so successfully inaugurated in this city, is indeed one fraught with interest to a large number of your readers.

Your correspondent of the 1st inst., oddly enough, makes this surprising confession — "My opinions may be old-fashioned, as well as quaint, concerning the rights of women. Years have obtused my mind and darkened my perceptions, yet, &c.," — seems to have here caught a faint conception of the very amusing spectacle presented in her contributions on this subject.

Happily life, we believe, to most young women of our day does not mean a mere romance of love — a holiday butterfly week — a wasteful blank. "The bright hopes of love's imaginations" are only kindled with a ten-fold more radiant beauty by the inspiration of a life of the highest usefulness — an ardent desire to do good. Every woman may not become a Florence Nightingale or a Miss Dix; but who can doubt that if the philanthropic labors of these noble women had been guided by proper medical acquirements, they would not have shone all the more lustrous and been of greater efficiency to those to whom they ministered.

As to the necessity, she impugns, of ladies studying and practising medicine, I, as a regular physician, with most of my colleagues in the profession, freely admit its urgency as of present vital moment to mankind. The more refined mankind becomes, the more pressing the need.

Volumes might be filled with the testimony of eminent writers, whose eyes have been opened to the glaring evils and the fearful havoc of the present system.

Prof. Meigs, confessedly one of the very best authorities says, in his treatise on the "Diseases of Females":

The relations between the sexes are of so delicate a character that the duties of the medical practitioner are necessarily more difficult when he comes to take charge of any one of the great host of female complaints than when he is called, to treat any of the more general disorders. So great indeed is the embarrassment, that I am persuaded that much of the ill success of treatment may be traced thereto.

All these evils of medical practice spring, not in the main, from any want of competency, in medicines or in medical men, but from the delicacy of the relations existing between the sexes, and in a good degree from a want of information among the population in general as to the importance and meaning, and tendency of disorders manifested by a certain train of symptoms.

It is, perhaps, best, upon the whole, that this great degree of modesty should exist, even to the extent of putting a bar to researches, without which no very clear and understandable notions can be obtained of the sexual disorders. I confess I am proud," he continues, "to say, that in this country, generally, certainly in many parts of it, there are women who prefer to suffer the extremity of danger and pain rather than waive those scruples of delicacy which prevent their maladies from being fully explored. I say it is an evidence of the dominion of a fine morality in society. Can anything be done to obviate the perpetuity of this evil — one that has existed for ages? Is there any resource by which the amount of suffering endured by women may be greatly lessened?

The remedy is perfectly natural and self-evident. Let us have properly qualified lady physicians. This demand the "Medical College for Women" is doing its utmost to meet.

Says the National Quarterly Review, of England, in arguing the necessity of a thorough medical education for women: "We believe women to be the most efficient and proper practitioners with their own sex." The late Thomas H. Benton remarked, "I think a matron physician should be attached to every seminary for the education of girls. Their own knowledge and experience would tell them when to make inquiries; and their motherly character would enable them to draw out revelations, before it should be too late, on which future health, or life itself, might depend."

"Mother of the Old School" asks what family would like to employ a lady as physician. Fortunately this question will regulate itself. The public governs the profession, not the profession it. Who in our day is obliged by law to employ any particular person as his physician! If, however, the medical colleges and hospitals are closed to women seeking instruction, the people will be absolutely compelled by the iron handed law of necessity to employ those whom they otherwise would not. It is true that because of the great demand in this direction, and the fact that our medical schools have been closed to women, some have ventured to practice with only a limited store of knowledge, thus bringing the cause into distrust. These have done some good as well as, doubtless, harm. Having by legislative charter and provision, established a high scientific school, there will be no excuse for the continuance of such ignorance. The interests of the people will be at once protected and advanced by it. If women are to practice medicine, and who can prevent it, it is not only right but safe that they should be thoroughly qualified.

It is not right either to fasten on woman tasks and employments for which she has no taste, or is unwilling to accept. If the extended practice of medicine prove too wearing, let her make it less so. If she do but little here, she will accomplish much.

Nor does this question involve that of women's rights, so called, nor the wearing of Bloomer costume, as is assumed. There is no good reason why lady physicians should not grace and refine any society in which they may move, by their superior endowment and the force of their noble nature. Indeed, many of these among us do already possess not only a highly honorable and remunerative practice, but are esteemed for their ever active philanthropy and generous self-sacrifice.

OBSERVER, NEW-YORK, FRIDAY, JAN. 6, 1865.

VIEWS OF A LADY PHYSICIAN.

To the Editor of the New-York Times:
After the complete refutation of the main arguments and assertions recently advanced in the TIMES by "Mother of the Old School," it was hoped that in her second public appearance she would have manifested a greater regard for consistency by avoiding statements equally unjustifiable and erroneous. She, however, still sadly misconceives, and therefore misrepresents the high position and character, not only of our students but of all our sex, by unlimited detraction of the noblest qualities, the most sacred and beautiful endowments everywhere conceded to be the peculiar attribute of refined womanhood.

According to her view, we ought to be debarred collegiate medical instruction and the art of healing, though thousands of our suffering sisters, stretching out their hands piteously imploring our aid, perish alas beneath our own gaze.

This touching appeal of woman for help, woman alone may hear and feel, and alone can remedy. It will be heard and felt so long as purity and modesty are the crowning excellencies of woman's character.

This she confidently affirms rises from a "mock-modesty, a false delicacy, that shuns the care and aid of a male practitioner."

Arraigned thus summarily before a self-constituted tribunal who reverses the decisions of all time, and accused of a morbid sensibility — a whimsical notion — we are expected to meekly submit to the enforcement of the harsh sentence pronounced by one of our own number, bear indignities, suffer martyrdom, loss of life itself, and the lose of those more dear than life; or,

"Pale about the fountain
Of their ancient freedom wait,
Till the angel move the waters
And avenge their stricken state."

Does your correspondent desire to express her very high estimate of the character of her own sex, by proclaiming her belief in the "gossiping propensities and prurient curiosity of women?" Does she think that our sex would, were we consulted, confide our fair fame to such keeping, or that we would judge that from her lips fall "the expression of warmest sympathy" for us?

Does she fancy, when she appeals to the unfair instincts of masculine jealousy, by the uncharitable remark that "woman was to be man's helpmeet, not his master," that she proves that the woman who, in obedience to the call of Christian duty, the highest impulse of the heart, asks the prerogative of an equal education, and is earnestly devoting herself to the salvation of her sex, is, by so doing, any the less "man's help-meet," or aspires to be his master?

Is not this continual assertion of man's superiority and woman's inferiority, quite as tiresome as it is useless to a cultivated community? Can the stream rise higher than its source? — manhood become elevated while woman is ignorant and degraded? Are not the interests of both inseparably linked together by the eternal laws of God?

When "Mother of the Old School" irreverently asks: "How dare feeble women to assume the awful responsibility of dealing with the lives of men?" she betrays ignorance of the plainest fact, that women have, willingly or unwillingly, the care of the human family, from the first dawn of existence to the last. Aye, more; she is the mother of the race. If she herself be sickly and imbecile, her offspring suffer the penalty. Why should she fold her hands and render herself or "her lot to bear, to nurse, to rear, to love, and then to lose," when by a little self-instruction and effort she can save those dear objects of her solicitude and care?

What means it, that, according to our statistics of mortality, almost one-fourth of the human race die before attaining the age of one year?

That before the age of five years, more than one-third of all who have been born have died, and one-half are supposed to have perished before attaining adult life?

Of those who survive to adult life, the sick and imbecile are a countless host; it is rare to find any person entirely free from all organic or functional disease. The most competent authorities agree that this fearful mortality is due to the physiological ignorance of wives and mothers.

This state of things, we claim, can and will be remedied by the success of our movement more than by any and all other means.

The noblest men and women in our midst bid us "God speed." The public, the pulpit, and the press are on our side. Our own hearts assure us that God's own hand is opening all the way before us.

LADY PHYSICIAN, NEW-YORK MEDICAL COLLEGE FOR WOMEN, NO. 724 BROADWAY, JAN. 7, 1865.

Equal Pay for Women.

BY THE NEW YORK TIMES | NOV. 12, 1916

MISSOULA, MONT., NOV. 11. — "I am going to Washington to represent the women and children of the West, to work for an eight-hour day for women and for laws providing that women shall receive the same wages as men for equal amounts of work," said Miss Jeanette Rankin, newly elected Republican member of Congress from Montana. She was sewing as she said this today. Even after entering politics she refused to forsake the old household arts, cooking, and needlework.

Miss Rankin refused to become excited when returns showed she was running ahead of the Republican ticket in Montana.

"I'm glad of this chance," was her comment when cheering friends brought the news. "Of course I know I'll be the first woman member of Congress, but I believe I'll be received with courtesy and as an equal by those Eastern Congressmen, even though they are enemies of suffrage. While working for suffrage in the East, I found that, no matter how strenuously our opponents fought us, they were always ready to hear our side."

In addition to her eight-hour day and equal wage laws, Miss Ranken intends to fight for woman suffrage from the moment she gets into the Capitol. Her suffrage bill, she says, will be one of the first introduced at the next session. She also declares her intention of seeking extension of the child labor laws, mothers' pensions and universal education.

An Olympic Figure Skater Who Also Made History for The Times

BY VICTOR MATHER | FEB. 21, 2018

MARIBEL VINSON is a revered name in American figure skating. She was a three-time Olympian, a bronze medalist behind the gold medalist Sonja Henie and an exacting coach who trained hundreds of young talents before dying in a plane crash in 1961.

But she had another distinction that is almost forgotten: Maribel Vinson was the first female sportswriter at The New York Times.

Vinson was already a magna cum laude Radcliffe graduate and a bronze medalist when she reported to work at The Times in 1934 at age 22. The Times was a different place then, a nearly all-male preserve. Women were still decorously referred to as "Miss" or "Mrs.," even in sports headlines.

There had been female reporters at the paper before, starting with Sara Jane Clarke, who wrote as Grace Greenwood in the 1850s. But their numbers were "pathetically meager," wrote Nan Robertson in her book "The Girls in the Balcony." And none of them had ever written for sports.

The sports editor at the time was Bernard William St. Denis Thomson, known in the office as the Colonel. (Gay Talese revealed in "The Kingdom and the Power" that he had actually been an army captain, not a colonel, and served in World War I as a trainer of pack animals.) Regardless of his rank, he was fond of barking orders to his underlings, military style.

He had hired Vinson "hesitantly and after considerable soul-searching," the Times columnist Arthur Daley wrote years later. "He regretted it the very first day" when he realized that he would not be able to swear as much.

Years later, though, Vinson recalled of her colleagues, "They soon found out I could outdrink them," according to one of her skating students, Frank Carroll (who would later coach some of the world's most renowned skaters).

Vinson was not just some celebrity author who swanned in to dash off a few skating articles. She plunged right into the daily grind of a real sportswriter. She amassed 189 bylines in her first 12 months, and covered track, tennis, swimming, lacrosse and horse shows.

Under the banner "Women in Sports," her first column reported on the Curtis Cup matches for amateur golfers and added notes about a fencing exhibition at the Hotel Astor and field hockey in Prospect Park.

Even at her young age, her prose reveals that she was a pro, seriously and carefully laying out the news of every event, even if it was low in the sports pecking order. Within the limits of The Times's strict rules and sometimes stiff house writing style, she managed to impart some flavor to her coverage.

In reporting on an outdoor swim meet in Manhattan Beach in 1935, she wrote, "It was not a water hazard but a mental hazard that Miss Rawls had to face in the medley race. For the sprightly, laughing Southerner is literally 'frightened to death' by lightning, and it must have been small comfort to see a telephone pole a block away struck by a bolt and burning merrily away."

Her bylines almost always appeared over accounts of women's sports. No one sent Vinson to write about a glamorous event like a bowl game, a prize fight or the World Series (although Carroll says she often attended such events with her male colleagues). Instead, she plied her trade at places like the Heights Casino in Brooklyn for squash, the Pelham Country Club for golf and Jones Beach for archery.

Daley acknowledged that while Vinson was "never completely accepted" by The Times's boys' club, she was eventually "warily admitted to the gang."

Amazingly, Vinson juggled full-time sportswriting with full-time athletic pursuits. On Jan. 13, 1936, she reported a squash story from the Cosmopolitan Club in Manhattan. On the 15th, she sailed for Germany and the Winter Olympics on the liner Washington. (It was an era when boat sailings were big news. The Times reported that Sergei Rachmaninoff was also on board; Vinson made the boat by just 10 minutes and forgot her uniform.)

On Feb. 2, her byline appeared again, over a story about the women's ski team. On the 13th, she finished fifth in her third Olympics. She also placed fifth in the pairs competition alongside George Hill. On March 3, she was back on the squash beat, reporting from London, and before the month was out she was back reporting on badminton from New York.

Vinson wrote her last article for the Times in 1937 ("Miss Amory Victor With Miss Phipps," on the results of a "Scotch foursome" golf match) and began her coaching career.

Vinson seldom got to show it in her articles about college field hockey, but she was an intellectual powerhouse. Carroll remembers that in the 1950s, "We drove around a lot to rinks and would discuss the philosophers I was studying at Holy Cross, like Thomas Aquinas. We'd talk about the Latin language, the differences between ecclesiastical Latin and classical Latin. She was one of the most brilliant women I've ever met."

They drove so much, Carroll notes, because Vinson was not allowed to teach at her home rink, the Skating Club of Boston. "She was brutal, and they didn't like that ... She was a very tough, tough mentor. She demanded discipline."

Vinson kept at writing, penning three books about figure skating and contributing off and on to The Associated Press and Boston Globe.

She raised two daughters, Maribel and Laurence, and both became elite skaters. (Laurence took after her mother and wrote poetry.) In 1961, mother and daughters, along with 15 other members of the U.S. skating team, died when their 707 jet crashed in Brussels on the way to the world championships in Prague. It was a devastating day for United States skating, and made front page news nationwide.

Vinson's legacy lives on through coaches like Carroll, who trained Michelle Kwan and Evan Lysacek, among others.

And through all the women sportswriters who have graced these pages.

Women Fitting Themselves Fast for Skilled Job in War Plants

BY ANNE PETERSEN | SEPT. 6, 1942

HOW SWIFTLY women are adapting themselves to the skills war industries demand is a story told in figures compiled by the United States Office of Education, showing a six-fold increase in their enrollment since February in engineering, chemistry, physics and production supervision courses. By the end of June new enrollments totaled 34,996, half of them distributed among colleges in five States near busy production centers — Pennsylvania, Texas, California, New York and Indiana.

The progress of women in a field which in ordinary times does not attract them in large numbers is receiving a partial test as a smaller group trained as engineering aides begins to take up posts in the drafting rooms where the parts for planes, ships and guns are drawn. These aides are the product of special new short courses set up under the auspices of the Office of Education, to fit women as assistants to engineers in testing laboratories, or in the planning departments of plane factories.

The courses, not ordinarily found in a college curriculum, were designed to fill the up-to-the-minute needs of the industries, and are given by special request of plant supervisors, who worked out details of instruction.

Success of this intense training is already reported from West Coast munition plants which have drawn on the class of thirty-five women who completed ten weeks at Stanford University in drafting and technical calculations.

In the Midwest, women were trained last Spring at the Illinois Institute of Technology for jobs in engineering, drafting inspection, testing and industrial chemistry. In the East, the testing department of General Electric Company at Schenectady has employed forty college women with a bent for physics and mathematics, and given them its own classroom and laboratory instruction.

At the Grumman Aircraft Corporation at Bethpage, L. I., Norma Victor and Nancy Chapman, two of nine young women trained at the plant, have just been made engineering aides, working on calculating machines in the test-flight and stress departments. Their number will be increased later this month, when a class of fifty-five completes a six-week course at Columbia University, worked out in a co-operative venture between the university and the plant. Candidates were chosen from 1,300 applicants by the firm's personnel department, for their adaptability to the work, not readily indicated by their former interests.

Miss Chapman, a graduate of Wells College, had majored in psychology at Barnard. A former student of archaeology, an interior designer, artists, illustrators and a large percentage of teachers are among the students.

The six-week course, from 9 to 5 daily, with home work, provides only the basic training for these potential draftsmen. At its conclusion they will get practical experience as shop mechanics for four months, combined with an advanced evening course.

Rose Gacioch, a Star in Women's Pro Baseball, Dies at 89

BY RICHARD GOLDSTEIN | SEPT. 16, 2004

ROSE GACIOCH, an outstanding outfielder and pitcher in the heyday of women's professional baseball who became a mainstay of the Rockford Peaches team later featured in the movie "A League of Their Own," died last Thursday at a nursing home in Clinton Township, Mich. She was 89.

Her death was announced by a niece, Helen Bozicevich.

Gacioch (pronounced GAY-sotch), a native of Wheeling, W.Va., was in grade school when she sneaked out of class to see Babe Ruth and Lou Gehrig play on a barnstorming stop, and she was thrilled when Gehrig shook her hand. At 16, she was the only girl on a town baseball team called the Little Cardinals.

While still in her teens, she played one season for the All Star Ranger Girls, a barnstorming women's team.

In 1944, after working in a West Virginia factory and playing softball, she joined the South Bend (Ind.) Blue Sox in the All-American Girls Baseball League, created the previous season by the Chicago Cubs' owner, Philip K. Wrigley, to provide entertainment if major league baseball was curtailed by World War II.

Gacioch played right field, and, as she told Susan E. Johnson in an interview for "When Women Played Hardball," she had a phenomenal assist total, thanks to a move by her manager, Bert Niehoff, a former National League infielder.

As she remembered it: "Bert said: 'Rose, I'm gonna put the second baseman closer to second, and the first baseman closer to first. Now you've got all that territory in between. Come in and flip the ball to first.' Batters would see a big space in right field, hit toward it. I'd run in, field the ball and throw them out at first. Twice in my career, I had 31 assists from right field, a league record."

Gacioch was sent to the Rockford (Ill.) Peaches the next year and played the outfield and pitched for them until the league folded after the 1954 season. She won 92 games and lost 60 and was a three-time All-Star, according to Ms. Johnson. She played on four championship teams with the Peaches.

Gacioch later worked in a factory in Rockford, retired in 1978, then lived in the Detroit area. She never married and is survived most immediately by three nieces.

Interest in women's baseball was revived long after the demise of the All-American Girls Baseball League. In 1988, the Hall of Fame created a Women in Baseball exhibit honoring the players of that league, and in 1992, "A League of Their Own," starring Madonna, Geena Davis, Rosie O'Donnell and Tom Hanks, provided a Hollywood version of the Peaches' exploits.

Gacioch visited Cooperstown for the exhibition opening and reveled in her niche at the Hall of Fame. As she said in the interview reflecting on her career: "I always say: 'Now I got something on Pete Rose. I got there before he did.' "

Gertrude Jeannette, Actor, Director and Cabdriver, Dies at 103

BY JONATHAN WOLFE | APRIL 26, 2018

ON HER FIRST DAY on the job, Gertrude Jeannette, believed to be the first woman to drive a cab in New York City, got in an accident — on purpose.

She had pulled up in front of the Waldorf-Astoria hotel in Manhattan looking for a fare but was cut off by other taxi drivers.

"In those days they didn't allow black drivers to work downtown; you had to work uptown," Ms. Jeannette, who was African-American, later recalled. "They said, 'Say, buddy, you know you're not supposed to be on this line.' "

As cabbies hurled insults and hemmed her in, she remained calmly on the line — until, that is, a Checker cab lurched in front of her.

"I rammed my fender under his fender, swung it over to the right and ripped it," she said in 2011 at a ceremony in her honor at the Dwyer Cultural Center in Harlem. When the other driver got a good look at her, she recalled, he screamed: "A woman driver! A woman driver!"

She was later reprimanded by an inspector, but she drove off with her very first customer.

Ms. Jeannette, who was also one of the first women to get a motorcycle license in New York, and who later overcame a speech impediment to become a Broadway, film and television actor as well as a playwright, producer and director, died on April 4 at her home in Harlem. She was 103.

Her niece Angela Hadley Brown confirmed the death.

Ms. Jeannette got her hack license in 1942. She had responded to an ad in a newspaper looking for women to replace the male cabdrivers who had been drafted into World War II.

"Women were going into plants and everything else, taking over jobs," she recalled in a 2005 interview. "I said, well, I know one thing — I can drive a car."

Gertrude Jeannette's taxi license from the late 1940s.

"Thirty-two of us took the test and only two of us passed," said Ms. Jeannette, who learned how to drive a Chrysler truck at the age of 13 in Arkansas. "But the other girl didn't get her license because she had citations on her driver's license. And so I, I was the first."

(Ms. Jeannette is widely thought to be the first woman to get a taxi license in New York City, said Allan Fromberg, the deputy commissioner for public affairs at the Taxi and Limousine Commission, but records from that period have been lost or destroyed. The first unlicensed female cabdriver in New York City was Wilma K. Russey in 1915.)

Ms. Jeannette never wanted to act, she said, but was pushed into the theater.

With the money she earned driving, she had set out to correct her childhood stammer by enrolling in the one speech class she could find, at the American Negro Theater, housed in the basement of what is today the Schomburg Center for Research in Black Culture in Harlem.

Acting instruction was part of the curriculum, and she studied alongside Sidney Poitier, Ruby Dee and Ossie Davis. She was quickly singled out for her stage presence and cast in her first Broadway production, "Lost in the Stars," which had its premiere at the Music Box Theater in 1949.

She would go on to land roles in Broadway productions like "The Long Dream" (1960), "Nobody Loves an Albatross" (1963), "The Amen Corner" (1965), "The Skin of Our Teeth" (1975) and "Vieux Carré" (1977), written by Tennessee Williams, with whom she became friends. Her film credits include "Cotton Comes to Harlem" (1970), "Shaft" (1971) and "Black Girl" (1972).

Ms. Jeannette began writing plays in 1950 in response to what she saw as an absence of authentic black characters on the stage.

"I saw parts that I knew I wouldn't play," she said in an interview in 1995. "And so I started writing about women, and strong women, that I knew that no one would be ashamed to play."

Gertrude Hadley was born on Nov. 28, 1914, in Urbana, Ark., about 15 miles from the Louisiana border. Her father, Willis Lawrence Hadley, taught at a mission on a Native American reservation near Spiro, Okla. Her mother, Salley Gertrude Crawford Hadley, was a homemaker.

Gertrude grew up on a farm with five brothers and one sister, climbing walnut trees, playing stickball and fishing for trout. During the Depression, she moved with her family to Little Rock, Ark., and enrolled at Dunbar High School, a segregated school, where she recalled beginning each day singing "Lift Every Voice and Sing."

On her prom night, she met her future husband, Joe Jeannette, a heavyweight prizefighter 35 years her senior, who was in town from New York. The pair danced the Lindy Hop, a popular dance in Harlem, and by the end of the song he had asked her to marry him.

"Just because I'm a small-town girl, I'm not a fool," she recalled telling him, in 2005. "And I walked off the floor."

He persisted, and they eloped to New York in 1933.

Mr. Jeannette was the president of the Harlem Dusters, a motorcycle club, and he taught his wife how to ride a motorcycle under the elevated train tracks (now demolished) on what is now Frederick Douglass Boulevard in Harlem.

"The 'el' train, they had these big pillars," she recalled. "And he would push me with no motor running, take the motorcycle and push me around, and have me to guide in and out those 'el' posts to get the swing of the motorcycle."

She got her motorcycle license in 1935, the same year she had her only son, Robert. He died at age 5.

Her husband worked as a bodyguard of sorts for Paul Robeson, the baritone singer, actor and political activist. In 1949, the Harlem Dusters, including Gertrude, traveled to what was to be an open-air concert in Peekskill, N.Y.

"That's the first time I saw the Ku Klux Klan," Ms. Jeannette recalled in 2015. "They came out to lynch Paul Robeson."

Klansmen set fire to crosses on the field, and American Legion members, protesting what they saw as Mr. Robeson's affinity for the Soviet Union and communism, clashed with concertgoers. The melee became known as the Peekskill Riots.

When the American Negro Theater closed in 1949, many of the company's black actors moved to California or elsewhere. Some, including Ms. Jeannette, were barred from working during the Red Scare of the 1950s; she was singled out, she said, because of her association with Mr. Robeson.

So Ms. Jeannette — "Mother Gertrude" or "Ms. J," as she was known in Harlem — set up a succession of theater companies in the neighborhood, including the H.A.D.L.E.Y. players (the letters stand for Harlem Artist's Development League Especially for You) in 1979.

"She had many opportunities to go to Hollywood, but she always stayed in Harlem," said Ward Nixon, who was the company's artistic director. "She stayed in Harlem to make sure the community had top-notch theater."

A demanding director, Ms. Jeannette mentored a generation of young black actors in New York. She wrote five plays, which grappled with racism, politics, family ties and the importance of education.

Her first, and her favorite, was "The Way Forward" (1950), which drew upon her childhood in Arkansas. In "A Bolt From the Blue," she explored the so-called Bronx Slave Market — groups of black women who huddled outside department stores searching for jobs as day laborers or domestic workers in the 1930s and '40s.

"They were wonderfully dramatic pieces, punctuated by lighter moments throughout," Mr. Nixon said of her work. "You always walked out of one of her plays feeling uplifted and encouraged."

She continued to act into her 80s and retired from directing at 98. Her husband died in 1956. She is survived by 10 nephews and 6 nieces.

"Ms. Jeannette left on this earth the feeling of hope," Mr. Nixon said. "That wherever you are in life, and whatever you want to do, you can always rise up."

Women's Job Bill Fought in Albany

BY LEONARD INGALLS | MARCH 14, 1964

ALBANY, MARCH 13 — Strong opposition from business and industry has threatened bills that would make it unlawful to discriminate against women in employment because of their sex.

Bills to protect women workers and provide for the investigation of complaints by the State Commission for Human Rights are pending in both the Senate and the Assembly. They have the backing of Attorney General Louis J. Lefkowitz and follow policies supported by Governor Rockefeller.

The business community has become alarmed by the proposals because they fear that they will lead to a disruption of business when complaints are investigated. They also contend that pension and insurance plans will be adversely affected.

The Empire State Chamber of Commerce, the Commerce and Industry Association and the New York Telephone Company are among the organizations that have recorded their opposition. They have communicated with Senator Thomas Laverne and Assemblyman J. Eugene Goddard, both Republicans of Rochester, who introduced the bills.

Another bill favored by the American Association of University Women and sponsored by the same legislators would declare it a civil right to obtain employment regardless of sex.

Where women are not physically able to perform a job, the proposed laws would permit their disqualification. Otherwise they would be entitled to equal opportunity in employment "unless a bona fide occupational reason can be shown for the discrimination."

Women are guaranteed equal pay for equal work under state law, but there is no present guarantee of full equality in employment.

The sponsors of the bills noted in a memorandum that 2.5 million women were employed in the state and made up almost a third of the total labor force of 7 million.

"By eliminating an outgrown and harmful prejudice," the sponsors said, "this bill would aid New York State in maintaining its leadership in the fields of social and economic progress."

"Unless women are guaranteed equal opportunity in hiring and promotion, equal pay for equal work, however worthy, does not provide them with full equality in employment."

Women's Pay Gap Is Still Widening, U.S. Official Says

BY THE NEW YORK TIMES | NOV. 15, 1964

WASHINGTON, NOV. 15 — The director of the Labor Department's Women's Bureau said today that the wage gap between men and women workers was widening, not narrowing.

According to the director, Mrs. Mary Dublin Keyserling, a 1963 comparison of the median earnings of the two sexes showed that women received an average of only 59 per cent of what men were paid on a full-time basis.

The most distressing thing about the wage gap, she said in a speech here, is that "it has been widening over the past 24 years in every major industry group in which large numbers of women are employed."

Added to this is a trend of the last 16 years in which women have become "increasingly, rather than less, concentrated in the lower-paid, less-skilled jobs," she said.

Last year, of 32 million women workers — 45 per cent of the women ages 18 to 64 — only half of 1 per cent earned more than $10,000. Only 3 per cent earned more than $7,000.

Mrs. Keyserling gave President Johnson credit for trying to reverse the trend.

From January to October, 1964, he appointed 68 women to top government jobs, she said. The executive agencies appointed 311 more women and promoted more than 1,230 women at salary levels of $10,000 a year or more.

The main barrier to promotion for women is prejudice, Mrs. Keyserling said.

"They are faced by myths, running entirely counter to facts, which assert that women make poor supervisors, or they have substantially higher rates of absenteeism and labor turnover," she said.

She Was the Only Woman in a Photo of 38 Scientists, and Now She's Been Identified

BY JACEY FORTIN | MARCH 19, 2018

LAST WEEK, hundreds of people were engaged in a search for a woman named Sheila.

It began when an illustrator's investigation into the archives of marine legislation turned into a very different kind of historical deep dive.

Candace Jean Andersen wanted to write a picture book about the Marine Mammal Protection Act of 1972, so she asked the National Oceanic and Atmospheric Administration for some information.

It sent her an article on the subject. There, buried in dozens of pages of dense text, was a photograph of attendees at the 1971 International Conference on the Biology of Whales in Virginia, a gathering of some of the most prominent experts in marine biology. The 38 people pictured appeared to be mostly white and all men, except for one: a young black woman wearing a bright headband, her face partly obscured by the man in front of her.

Ms. Andersen said the men were named in a caption but the woman was not. "My curiosity nagged at me, not knowing who the woman in the photo was, or perhaps what she may have contributed to the conference," she said.

How do you identify a person when all you have is half of a smiling face in a 47-year-old black-and-white photo?

You turn to social media.

"Hey Twitter," Ms. Andersen wrote in a post on March 9. "I'm on a mission."

After she posted the photo, hundreds of people replied with comments and suggestions.

The thread caught the attention of Margot Lee Shetterly, the author of the book "Hidden Figures: The American Dream and the Untold Story of the Black Women Mathematicians Who Helped Win the Space Race."

"Here's a working scientist, contributing alongside her colleagues, and she's not even given the professional courtesy of having her name recorded at a scientific conference," Ms. Shetterly said on Sunday. "The photo, with her brown face half obscured by the people around her, is a perfect metaphor for the larger issue of history's failure to record the work of women scientists, particularly women scientists of color."

Inspired by Ms. Andersen's post, amateur researchers began combing through historical records and unearthing the names of women who worked in the sciences during the 1970s.

Maybe, some suggested, the photo was of the oceanographer, professor and lawyer Matilene Spencer Berryman, who died in 2003? Or perhaps it was Suzanne Contos, who helped organize the conference in 1971? (It was neither. Ms. Berryman's age did not seem to match the photo, and Ms. Contos said it was not her.)

Then Dee Allen, the research program officer at the Marine Mammal Commission, saw the photograph on Twitter and contacted some of her mentors.

"I figured it was probably something I could track down pretty easily, and I have an appreciation for the history of the field," Ms. Allen said. She contacted Don Wilson, the emeritus curator of mammals at the Smithsonian National Museum of Natural History.

Dr. Wilson remembered. He told Ms. Allen that the woman had worked as a museum technician, and her name was Sheila.

"Sheila was working at the museum in the Division of Mammals when I first started there in September 1971," Dr. Wilson said, adding that she was "an excellent technician."

Ms. Allen gave the information to Ms. Andersen, who began to look for Sheila on social media.

By March 12, she had found her. Ms. Andersen revealed that Sheila's original surname was Minor and posted snippets of their conversation, in which she said she had worked in several federal agencies for 35 years and "loved every moment of my career."

The discovery was cheered by Ms. Andersen's Twitter followers, and by Ms. Shetterly, who said it was "critically important" to tell the stories of people like Sheila who have historically been underrepresented, "as the leaky pipeline exists in the history of science and technology as well as in its present."

On Sunday, Sheila said her full name is Sheila Minor Huff. She is a retired, 71-year-old grandmother of five who belly dances, volunteers at her church and lives in Virginia.

Ms. Huff said she began working as an animal technician shortly after graduating with a bachelor's degree in biology. When she applied for her first job at the Bureau of Sport Fisheries and Wildlife, she was asked to work as a typist. "I said, 'No, I went to school too long to be your secretary!' " she recalled.

Ms. Huff said she went on to complete a master's degree while working full time. She went to the Soviet Union to attend a conference for mammalogists. She worked with top government officials on a range of wildlife and environmental projects. By the time she retired, at 58, she had become a GS-14 federal employee — one of the highest designations possible — at the Department of the Interior.

She said she was not too bothered about going unnamed in the 1971 snapshot.

"It's kind of like, no big deal," she said. "When I try to do good, when I try and add back to this wonderful earth that we have, when I try to protect it, does it matter that anybody knows my name?"

Female-Run Venture Capital Funds Alter the Status Quo

BY CLAIRE CAIN MILLER | APRIL 1, 2015

STEP INTO THE offices on Sand Hill Road, the heart of Silicon Valley venture capital, and one thing is immediately striking — the almost all-male cast of leading characters.

But there is another corner of the venture capital industry that looks quite different. There, women run firms, and all-female networks of angel investors share deal opportunities and advise one another on investments.

This new group of firms and angel networks — including Cowboy Ventures, Aspect Ventures, Broadway Angels, Illuminate Ventures, Forerunner Ventures and Aligned Partners — stands in stark contrast to the rest of the industry.

In some ways, these new female-dominated firms and investment networks are a sign of success. There are now enough experienced, financially successful women to start their own firms, the way men with last names like Kleiner and Draper did in the past. In March, six women who are current or former Twitter executives announced #Angels, a new angel investing network.

In addition to having significant investing or operations experience, the women offer a broader and more diverse network for recruiting and finding new start-ups and an understanding of female consumers, who are often the dominant users of new products.

"We're in the middle of a shifting trend where there are newly wealthy women putting their money to work, and similarly we're starting to have a larger number of experienced investors," said Jennifer Fonstad, a founder of Aspect Ventures and Broadway Angels, who was formerly a partner at Draper Fisher Jurvetson. "Venture women are going out and doing what we saw a lot of the guys do."

PETER DASILVA FOR THE NEW YORK TIMES

Theresia Gouw, left, and Jennifer Fonstad are co-founders of Aspect Ventures, one of a growing number of venture capital firms led by women.

But it is also a sign of the deep-seated problems in the venture capital industry. A recent gender-discrimination trial — in which Ellen Pao, a former junior partner at Kleiner Perkins Caufield & Byers, sued the firm — exposed elements of a male-dominated culture in which women are sorely underrepresented. Over all, just 6 percent of partners at venture capital firms are women, according to the Diana Project at Babson College. That is even lower than in 1999, when 10 percent were female. And, according to another study of gender and venture capital, 77 percent of the firms have never had a female investor.

That study, by Paul A. Gompers, a professor of business administration at Harvard Business School, found that a lack of inclusion and mentorship by male partners hurts female partners in a material way, by driving down their overall returns.

"What's clear from these results is that investment returns are not only related to your own track record, but to having good colleagues around you," said Professor Gompers, who was a paid witness for the defense in the discrimination trial, which Ms. Pao lost. "And the surprising thing is, on average, women aren't benefiting from their male colleagues."

Venture capitalists are, in a way, the gatekeepers to Silicon Valley, and if they are a group of white men who studied at places like Stanford, it is no wonder that most of the entrepreneurs fit the same mold. Venture firms with women as partners are three times as likely to invest in a company with a female chief executive and twice as likely to invest in one with women on the management team, according to the Babson College report.

The lack of female investors has cascading effects. Start-ups' boards are composed mostly of venture capitalists, so they are often all men. A recent Fortune analysis found that of the 81 start-ups worth more than $1 billion, 5 percent had a female chief executive and 6 percent had a woman on the board. Other studies have found that male founders and directors are less likely to hire women as executives and engineers, or pay men and women equally.

"Honestly, there will be more female entrepreneurs if there are more female venture capitalists," said Brit Morin, founder and chief executive of an e-commerce and crafts site called Brit & Co, whose investors include Cowboy Ventures.

Female investors said they did not specifically seek to invest in companies founded by women, but that because of their networks, they received more pitches from female entrepreneurs. Forty percent of the angel investments made by Sonja Hoel Perkins, a founder of Broadway Angels (not related to Tom Perkins, the co-founder of Kleiner Perkins), have been in companies started by women, a far greater proportion than are made by typical venture funds. That is also the case with a third of Cowboy Ventures' 30 investments, and more than 40 percent of Aspect Ventures' 13 investments.

"We are getting a first look at an unfair share of these amazing, oftentimes repeat entrepreneurs, who happen to be female," said Theresia Gouw, a founder of Aspect and a former partner at Accel. Since more than half of the users of many mobile and social services are women, she added, companies can benefit from having female investors evaluate their products and serve on their boards.

That has been true for Mariam Naficy, the founder and chief executive of Minted, a crowd-sourced marketplace for stationery and art that has raised $89 million. Early in her company's life, before there was data to prove that her idea was a good one, female investors were much more likely than men to understand it, she said.

"Without being able to see quantitative evidence of better design, most male investors couldn't allow themselves to make the leap," Ms. Naficy said. "To virtually every female investor I met with, it was clear Minted's community was producing far fresher and more unique design than our competitors."

That seems to be paying off for Ms. Perkins, who was an early investor in Minted and said it is on track to being worth $1 billion.

Not that female venture capitalists invest only in companies with predominantly female customers. "There's a myth out there that

PETER DASILVA FOR THE NEW YORK TIMES

Forty percent of the angel investments made by Sonja Hoel Perkins have been in companies started by other women.

women only know how to invest in women's products," said Cindy Padnos, founder of Illuminate Ventures. She invests in cloud and mobile services for businesses.

"Women say, 'If there were more women founders, I would invest in more of them,' " she said. "That's too easy an excuse. You have to go out of your way to identify them and be receptive and show them this is a place where women and men succeed."

Many of the women who have started the new firms said they did it because after spending so much time with entrepreneurs, they wanted to create their own start-ups. Because many traditional venture funds have ballooned and expanded to late-stage and international companies, there was a need for new, smaller investors who were focused on financing early-stage companies.

"We are in a valley of people who challenge the status quo, so it sort of seems natural that we have venture investors who are thinking about how to do things differently," said Aileen Lee, founder of Cowboy Ventures and a former partner at Kleiner Perkins.

But most of all, Ms. Perkins said, working with women seemed fun. "All of us thought it would be great to be only women because all of us had worked with only men our whole lives," she said.

"I also thought it would be inspiring for women and girls to get into venture capital and technology," she added, "because I think a lot of women think, 'Why be in venture capital if you perceive the industry as not being friendly toward you?' "

All Combat Roles Now Open to Women, Defense Secretary Says

BY MATTHEW ROSENBERG AND DAVE PHILIPPS | DEC. 3, 2015

IN A HISTORIC transformation of the American military, Defense Secretary Ashton B. Carter said on Thursday that the Pentagon would open all combat jobs to women.

"There will be no exceptions," Mr. Carter said at a news conference. He added, "They'll be allowed to drive tanks, fire mortars and lead infantry soldiers into combat. They'll be able to serve as Army Rangers and Green Berets, Navy SEALs, Marine Corps infantry, Air Force parajumpers and everything else that was previously open only to men."

The groundbreaking decision overturns a longstanding rule that had restricted women from combat roles, even though women have often found themselves in combat in Iraq and Afghanistan over the past 14 years.

It is the latest in a long march of inclusive steps by the military, including racial integration in 1948 and the lifting of the ban on gay men and lesbians serving openly in the military in 2011. The decision this week will open about 220,000 military jobs to women.

The military faced a deadline set by the Obama administration three years ago to integrate women into all combat jobs by January or ask for specific exemptions. The Navy and Air Force have already opened almost all combat positions to women, and the Army has increasingly integrated its forces.

The announcement Thursday was a rebuke to the Marine Corps, which has a 93 percent male force dominated by infantry and a culture that still segregates recruits by gender for basic training. In September, the Marines requested an exemption for infantry and armor positions, citing a yearlong study that showed integration could hurt its fighting ability. But Mr. Carter said he overruled the Marines because the military should operate under a common set of standards.

Gen. Joseph E. Dunford Jr., the former commandant of the Marine Corps who recently became chairman of the Joint Chiefs of Staff, did not attend the announcement, and in a statement Thursday appeared to give only tepid support, saying, "I have had the opportunity to provide my advice on the issue of full integration of women into the armed forces. In the wake of the secretary's decision, my responsibility is to ensure his decision is properly implemented."

Women have long chafed under the combat restrictions, which allowed them to serve in combat zones, often under fire, but prevented them from officially holding combat positions, including in the infantry, which remain crucial to career advancement. Women have long said that by not recognizing their real service, the military has unfairly held them back.

A major barrier fell this year when women were permitted to go through the grueling training that would allow them to qualify as Army Rangers, the service's elite infantry.

Mr. Carter said that women would be allowed to serve in all military combat roles by early next year. He characterized the change as necessary to ensure that the United States military remained the world's most powerful.

"When I became secretary of defense, I made a commitment to building America's force of the future," Mr. Carter told reporters. "In the 21st century that requires drawing strength from the broadest possible pool of talent. This includes women."

Many women hailed the decision. "I'm overjoyed," said Katelyn van Dam, an attack helicopter pilot in the Marine Corps who has deployed to Afghanistan. "Now if there is some little girl who wants to be a tanker, no one can tell her she can't."

But the Republican chairmen of the Senate and House Armed Services Committees expressed caution and noted that by law Congress had 30 days to review the decision.

"Secretary Carter's decision to open all combat positions to women will have a consequential impact on our service members and our

LYNSEY ADDARIO FOR THE NEW YORK TIMES

Cpl. Christina Oliver, 25, a United States Marine with the Female Engagement Team, patrolled near an Afghan village to clear the area of Taliban in 2010.

military's warfighting capabilities," Senator John McCain of Arizona and Representative Mac Thornberry of Texas said in a statement. "The Senate and House Armed Services Committees intend to carefully and thoroughly review all relevant documentation related to today's decision."

Some in the military have privately voiced concern that integration will prove impractical, especially in the infantry, where heavy loads and long periods of deprivation are part of the job.

"Humping a hundred pounds, man, that ain't easy, and it remains the defining physical requirement of the infantry," said Paul Davis, an exercise scientist who did a multiyear study of the Marine infantry. "The practical reality is that even though we want to knock down this last bastion of exclusion, the preponderance of women will not be able to do the job."

Mr. Carter acknowledged at the news conference that simply opening up combat roles to women was not going to lead to a fully integrated military. Senior defense officials and military officers would have to overcome the perception among many service members, men and women alike, that the change would reduce the effectiveness of the armed services.

The defense secretary sought to assuage those concerns on Thursday by saying that every service member would have to meet the standards of the jobs they wished to fill, and "there must be no quotas or perception thereof."

He also acknowledged that many units were likely to remain largely male, especially elite infantry troops and Special Operations forces, where "only small numbers of women could" likely meet the standards.

"Studies say there are physical differences," Mr. Carter said, though he added that some women could meet the most demanding physical requirements, just as some men could not.

At the same time, he said, military leaders are going to be required to assign jobs and tasks and determine who is promoted based on "ability, not gender."

Lt. Col. Kate Germano, who oversaw the training of female recruits for the Marines until she was removed this summer from duty during a dispute over what she said were lower standards for women in basic training, said by creating standards, the military would improve across both genders.

She said while Marines have long resisted the idea of women in combat units, she did not expect a backlash.

"One thing about the Marine Corps, once you tell us what we have to do, we'll do it," she said. "There was resistance to lifting the ban on gays, too, and when it was lifted there were no issues. We are a stronger force for it."

Mr. Carter's announcement came less than a month from the three-year deadline set by the Obama administration to integrate the force.

Some veterans of recent wars say the unexpectedly long period of combat with no clear enemy lines may have been a driver for the change.

"I honestly didn't think about women in combat much until Iraq," said Jonathan Silk, a retired Army major who served in Afghanistan and Iraq as a cavalry scout.

In the fray of the insurgency, he said, integrated military police units near him often faced ferocious attacks. "That is where I encountered female soldiers that were in the same firefights as us, facing the same horrible stuff, even if they weren't technically in combat units. They could fight just as well as I could, and some of those women were tremendous leaders. It gave me such respect."

When the Pilot Is a Mom: Accommodating New Motherhood at 30,000 Feet

BY ANNALYN KURTZ | AUG. 16, 2016

BOARDING A FLIGHT can feel like stepping into a time capsule — men typically fly the plane, while most flight attendants are still women. Which is why a female pilot from Delta Air Lines did something dramatic at a union meeting recently.

Standing before her male colleagues, the captain unbuttoned her uniform, strapped a breast pump over the white undershirt she wore underneath, and began to demonstrate the apparatus. As the machine made its typical "chug, chug, chug" noise, attendees squirmed in their seats, looked at their feet and shuffled papers.

It was the latest episode in what has proved to be a difficult workplace issue to solve: how to accommodate commercial airline pilots who are balancing new motherhood.

It is a question that some employers have answered by creating leave policies or lactation rooms. But the flight deck of a jumbo jet isn't a typical workplace. Pilots are exempt from a provision in the Affordable Care Act requiring employers to accommodate new mothers. At 30,000 feet, the issue touches not only on pilot privacy, but also aircraft safety.

At Delta, a group of women pilots have banded together through a private Facebook page and have approached their union with formal proposals for paid maternity leave — unheard-of at the major airlines — because they say they would like to stay home to breast-feed their babies. At Frontier Airlines, four female pilots are suing the company for discrimination, seeking the option of temporary assignments on the ground while pregnant or nursing.

While their proposals differ, all say they aim for one thing: to avoid situations in which pilots have been leaving the cockpit in midflight

THEO STROOMER FOR THE NEW YORK TIMES

First Officer Brandy Beck, a pilot for Frontier Airlines, at home with her children in Denver this month.

for as long as 20 minutes, the amount of time often required to pump breast milk.

"The airlines have maternity policies that are archaic," said Kathy McCullough, 61, a retired captain for Northwest Airlines, which merged with Delta in 2008, who has advocated on behalf of the pilots to Delta management. "I am so glad that they're stepping forward and taking a stand."

One reason for the lack of rules is that women make up only about 4 percent of the nation's 159,000 certified airline pilots — a number that has been slow to rise over the past decade or so.

There were no female pilots at the biggest airlines until 1973, when American Airlines hired the first, Bonnie Tiburzi Caputo. In a reminder of how times have changed, that news was reported in The Los Angeles Times under the headline, "Airline Pilot to Fly by Seat of Panties."

"Airline jobs were really reserved for men," said Captain Caputo,

67, who became something of a minor celebrity when American hired her. She has been retired from the airline for about 18 years. "When we started, there were no maternity leaves, because there were no female pilots."

More than 40 years later, the major carriers still haven't resolved this issue. They set their policies for pilots based on the collective bargaining agreements negotiated by the unions. But women of child-bearing age account for just a sliver of union membership, so maternity leave and breast-feeding policies have not been at the top of union agendas.

Plus, some members oppose the proposals, citing the costs. One local union leader told several women in an email: "Having a child is a personal choice and asking the rest of us to fund your choice will be a difficult sell to the pilot group." The leader declined to be interviewed for this article; the union said he was not an authorized spokesman.

Delta's female pilots still hope to win over a majority of their colleagues. They argue that without paid leave, they're faced with a choice to either stay home to breast-feed their babies or earn income for their families.

Push for Gender Equality in Tech? Some Men Say It's Gone Too Far

BY NELLIE BOWLES | SEPT. 23, 2017

After revelations of harassment and bias in Silicon Valley, a backlash is growing against the women in tech movement.

SAN FRANCISCO — Their complaints flow on Reddit forums, on video game message boards, on private Facebook pages and across Twitter. They argue for everything from male separatism to an end to gender diversity efforts.

Silicon Valley has for years accommodated a fringe element of men who say women are ruining the tech world.

Now, as the nation's technology capital — long identified as one of the more hostile work environments for women — reels from a series of high-profile sexual harassment and discrimination scandals, these conversations are gaining broader traction.

One of those who said there had been a change is James Altizer, an engineer at the chip maker Nvidia. Mr. Altizer, 52, said he had realized a few years ago that feminists in Silicon Valley had formed a cabal whose goal was to subjugate men. At the time, he said, he was one of the few with that view.

Now Mr. Altizer said he was less alone. "There's quite a few people going through that in Silicon Valley right now," he said. "It's exploding. It's mostly young men, younger than me."

Mr. Altizer said that a gathering he hosts in person and online to discuss men's issues had grown by a few dozen members this year to more than 200, that the private Facebook pages he frequents on men's rights were gaining new members and that a radical subculture calling for total male separatism was emerging.

"It's a witch hunt," he said in a phone interview, contending men are being fired by "dangerous" human resources departments. "I'm

JASON HENRY FOR THE NEW YORK TIMES

James Damore was fired by Google last month after suggesting that there may be biological reasons for gender gaps in tech jobs.

sitting in a soundproof booth right now because I'm afraid someone will hear me. When you're discussing gender issues, it's almost religious, the response. It's almost zealotry."

Mr. Altizer is part of a backlash against the women in technology movement. While many in the tech industry had previously dismissed the fringe men's rights arguments, some investors, executives and engineers are now listening. Though studies and surveys show there is no denying the travails women face in the male-dominated industry, some said that the line for what counted as harassment had become too easy to cross and that the push for gender parity was too extreme a goal. Few were willing to talk openly about their thinking, for fear of standing out in largely progressive Silicon Valley.

Even so, "witch hunt" is the new whispered meme. Some in tech have started identifying as "contrarians," to indicate subtly that they do not follow the "diversity dogma." And self-described men's rights

CHRISTIE HEMM KLOK FOR THE NEW YORK TIMES

Google's main campus in Mountain View, Calif. "What Google did was wake up sectors of society that weren't into these issues before," said Paul Elam, who runs a men's rights group.

activists in Silicon Valley said their numbers at meetings were rising.

Others are playing down the women-in-tech issue. Onstage at a recent event, the venture capitalist Vinod Khosla said harassment in Silicon Valley was "rarer than in most other businesses."

Many men now feel like "there's a gun to the head" to be better about gender issues, said Rebecca Lynn, a venture capitalist at Canvas Ventures, and while "there's a high awareness right now, which is positive, at the same time there's a fear."

The backlash follows increasingly vulgar harassment revelations in Silicon Valley. Several female engineers and entrepreneurs this year named the men they accused of harassing them, and suddenly tech's boys' club seemed anything but impervious. Travis Kalanick, Uber's co-founder, resigned as chief executive after the ride-hailing service was embroiled in harassment accusations. Dave McClure, head of the incubator 500 Startups, called himself "a creep" and stepped down.

This month, the chief executive of Social Finance, Mike Cagney, also quit amid a harassment scandal.

In the aftermath, many stood up for gender equality in tech. Reid Hoffman, LinkedIn's founder, asked investors to sign a "decency pledge." Many companies reiterated that they needed to improve work force diversity.

"In just the last 48 hours, I've spoken to a female tech executive who was grabbed by a male C.E.O. at a large event and another female executive who was asked to interview at a venture fund because they 'feel like they need to hire a woman,' " said Dick Costolo, the former chief of Twitter, who now runs the fitness start-up Chorus. "We should worry about whether the women-in-tech movement has gone too far sometime after a couple of these aren't regularly happening anymore."

But those who privately thought things had gone too far were given a voice by James Damore, 28, a soft-spoken Google engineer. Mr. Damore, frustrated after another diversity training, wrote a memo that he posted to an internal Google message board. In it, he argued that maybe women were not equally represented in tech because they were biologically less capable of engineering. Google fired him last month.

After months of apologizing by Silicon Valley for bad behavior, here was a young man whom some in tech's leadership could potentially get behind.

Paul Graham, who founded an influential start-up incubator, Y Combinator, posted two articles about how the science behind Mr. Damore's memo was accurate. Another start-up investor, John Durant, wrote that "Charles Darwin himself would be fired from Google for his views on the sexes."

And the investor Peter Thiel's business partner, Eric Weinstein, tweeted, "Dear @Google, Stop teaching my girl that her path to financial freedom lies not in coding but in complaining to HR."

Mr. Durant declined to comment. Mr. Graham said in an email that there needed to be more distinction between fact and policy, and Mr. Weinstein said there was "a sea of brilliant women" and that more

JASON HENRY FOR THE NEW YORK TIMES

The push for gender equality "created divides that I didn't anticipate," said Joelle Emerson, next to the screen at a meeting in San Francisco. Her company, Paradigm, designs diversity strategies.

needed to be done to "figure out how to more fully empower them."

Now men's rights advocates in Silicon Valley have galvanized.

"What Google did was wake up sectors of society that weren't into these issues before," said Paul Elam, who runs A Voice for Men, a men's rights group. He said his organization had seen more interest from people in Silicon Valley.

Silicon Valley has always been a men's space, others said. Warren Farrell, who lives in Marin County, Calif., and whose 1993 book, "The Myth of Male Power," birthed the modern men's rights movement, said, "The less safe the environment is for men, the more they will seek little pods of safety like the tech world."

This turn in the gender conversation is good news for Mr. Damore. "The emperor is naked," he said in an interview. "Since someone said it, now it's become sort of acceptable."

He added, "The whole idea that diversity improves workplace output, it's not scientifically decided that that's true."

Mr. Damore filed a labor complaint against Google in August and said more than 20 people had reached out about joining together for a class-action suit about systemic discrimination against men. He is represented by Harmeet Dhillon, a local firebrand lawyer.

"It's become fashionable in Silicon Valley for people like James, a white man, to be put into a category of less desirable for promotion and advancement," Ms. Dhillon said. "Some companies have hiring goals like 'We'll give you a bonus if you're a hiring manager and you hire 70 percent women to this organization.' That's illegal."

Google declined to comment.

Two men who worked at Yahoo sued the company for gender discrimination last year. Their lawyer, Jon Parsons, said the female leadership — Yahoo's chief executive was Marissa Mayer, before Verizon bought the company — had gone too far in trying to hire and promote women. He tied the suit into today's women-in-tech movement.

"When you're on a mission from God to set the world straight, it's easy to go too far," Mr. Parsons said. "There was no control over women hiring women."

He said that his clients, Greg Anderson and Scott Ard, had faced gender discrimination in Yahoo's media teams and that other teams like cars were headed by women, which to Mr. Parsons was a sign of problems.

"No eyebrows are going to rise if a woman heads up fashion," Mr. Parsons said. "But we're talking about women staffing positions — things like autos — where it cannot be explained other than manipulation."

Those leading Silicon Valley's gender equality push said they were astonished that just as the movement was having an impact, it opened up an even more radical men's rights perspective.

"It's exhausting," said Joelle Emerson, who runs Paradigm, a company that designs diversity strategies. "It's created divides that I didn't anticipate."

One radical fringe that is growing is Mgtow, which stands for Men Going Their Own Way and pronounced MIG-tow. Mgtow aims for total male separatism, including forgoing children, avoiding marriage and limiting involvement with women. Its message boards are brimming with activity from Silicon Valley, Mr. Altizer said.

Cassie Jaye, who lives in Marin County and made a documentary about the men's rights movement called "The Red Pill," said that the tech world and the men's rights community had "snowballed" together and that the rise in the number of people in Mgtow is new.

On the Mgtow message boards, members discuss work ("Ever work for a woman? Roll up your sleeves and share your horror story"), technology ("The stuff girlfriends and wives can't stand — computers, games, consoles") and dating (mostly best practices to avoid commitment).

"I think there are a lot of guys living this lifestyle without naming it, and then they find Mgtow," said Ms. Jaye, who calls herself a former feminist.

Mr. Altizer leads Bay Area Fathers' Rights, a monthly support group for men to talk about the issues they uniquely face. He became interested in the community after a divorce and said his eyes were opened to how few rights men have. As for the numbers of women in tech, the effort for parity is absurd, he said.

"I've been on the hiring side for years," Mr. Altizer said, adding that he is not currently hiring people. "It would be nice to have women, but you cannot find applicants."

CHAPTER 4

In Politics

One of the most consequential roles in society is that of pol-
itician. Elected leaders shape the legislation that determines
how society functions. In the United States, the first woman
elected to Congress was Jeanette Rankin in 1917 — three
years before women won the right to vote! Fifty years later,
Shirley Chisholm became the first black woman elected to
Congress. Both women fought to change laws to improve
the lives of women. Vice-presidental candidate Geraldine
Ferraro laid the groundwork in 1984 for Hillary Clinton's
presidential run in 2016. And Hillary Clinton's loss at the
polls motivated record numbers of women to run for office
at all levels of government.

Women Greet Miss Rankin.

BY THE NEW YORK TIMES | APRIL 3, 1917

WASHINGTON, APRIL 2. — Representative Jeanette Rankin of Montana,
the first woman member of Congress, took her seat In the House today
after an elaborate prelude of ceremonies, in which woman suffragists
predominated. The principal occasion was a breakfast for "the Honorable Jeanette Rankin of Montana," under the auspices of suffragists of
all factions.

Mrs. Carrie Chapman Catt, President of the National American
Woman Suffrage Association, sat at Miss Rankin's right and at her
left was Miss Alice Raul, Chairman of the National Women's Party.
"The day of our deliverance is at hand," was the keynote of Mrs. Catt's
speech to the notable gathering of women. Miss Rankin, in reply, made

the longest speech she has delivered since her arrival in the Capital.

"The day after election," said Miss Rankin. "It looked very much as if I had not been elected, but it seemed to me that the campaign had been nevertheless worth while because the women had stood together, the women had learned solidarity. It seemed to me that that one thing had been alone worth striving for. I think that this breakfast this morning shows that the women are standing together.

"I want you to know how much I feel this responsibility. There will be many times when I shall make mistakes and it means a great deal to me to know that I have your encouragement and support."

Mrs. Chisholm Defeats Farmer, Is First Negro Woman in House

BY RICHARD L. MADDEN | NOV. 6, 1968

DEMOCRATS WON two normally Republican House seats in New York City yesterday and also elected Mrs. Shirley Chisholm the first Negro woman member of Congress.

Mrs. Chisholm, the Democratic National Committeewoman from New York, defeated James L. Farmer, a former head of the Congress of Racial Equality and the Liberal-Republican candidate. She won by about a 2-to-l margin in the newly drawn 12th Congressional District in the Bedford-Stuyvesant section of Brooklyn.

For the first time since 1936, a Democrat — City Councilman Edward I. Koch — won in the 17th Congressional District on Manhattan's East Side, which was represented by John V. Lindsay before his election as Mayor in 1965. With the returns nearly complete Mr. Koch led State Senator Whitney North Seymour Jr., a Republican, by about 14,000 votes and Mr. Seymour appeared at the Koch headquarters shortly before midnight to concede defeat.

The Democrats gained another House seat in the 24th Congressional District in the Northeast Bronx where Mario Biaggi, a much-decorated retired police lieutenant, won the seat vacated after 16 years by Paul A. Fino, a Republican who was elected to the state Supreme Court.

Mr. Biaggi, who also had Conservative party endorsement, defeated Andrew P. Mantovani, a Republican and administrative assistant to Mr. Fino, by more than 22,000 votes.

One Democratic incumbent, Representative John G. Dow of Grand View, an early critic of the Administration's conduct of the war in Vietnam, was defeated by his Republican challenger. Martin B. McKneally of Newburgh, a former national commander of the American Legion in the four-county 27th Congressional District northwest of New York City.

BETTMANN

Shirley Chisholm gives the victory sign after winning the Congressional election in Brooklyn's 12th District. She defeated civil rights leader James Farmer to become the first African American woman elected to Congress.

In the 28th Congressional District in the mid-Hudson Valley, John S. Dyson, a 25-year-old Millbrook newspaper publisher and a Democrat, held a slight lead over Hamilton Fish Jr., a Republican, for the House seat formerly held by Representative Joseph Y. Resnick, a Democrat. Going into yesterday's election, the Democrats had a majority of New York's 41 House seats, with 25 Democrats, 15 Republicans and one vacancy.

That vacancy was filled again by Adam Clayton Powell, a Democrat, who easily won re-election from the 18th Congressional District in Harlem.

Mr. Powell was excluded from the House in March, 1967, on the ground that he misused public funds and had defied New York court orders arising from a defamation suit. He was re-elected to the House later in a special election but did not claim his seat because of a continuing court battle.

EDDIE HAUSNER/THE NEW YORK TIMES

Edward I. Koch, Democrat, at his 17th District center.

Mr. Powell, who did almost no campaigning for re-election, had said that he will attempt to claim his seat after this election.

In upstate New York, two incumbent Democrats in normally Republican districts were re-elected despite strong challenges. In Syracuse, James M. Hanley, the two-term Incumbent Democrat, defeated David V. O'Brien, the Republican. And in the 35th Congressional District in central New York, Representative Samuel S. Stratton, a Democrat, defeated former state Senator George R. Metcalf, a Republican.

Representative Daniel E. Button, a Republican who won an upset victory two years ago in the 29th Congressional District, won re-election despite a strong campaign from the Albany Democratic organization and Jacob H. Herzog, the Democratic-Conservative candidate.

In the 38th Congressional District in Western New York, State Senator James F. Hastings, a Republican, easily won election to succeed Charles E. Goodell, a Republican, who was appointed United States Senator to succeed Robert F. Kennedy.

A new House seat was at stake in the race between Mrs. Chisholm and Mr. Farmer. The new district, the 12th Congressional District in Brooklyn, was drawn by the Legislature last year and takes in the Bedford-Stuyvesant section, one of the nation's largest Negro slums.

Mrs. Chisholm, who campaigned as an "unbought and unbossed" candidate, spent four years in the state Assembly and last August was elected as the Democratic National Committeewoman from New York State.

Mr. Farmer, a Liberal who had Republican endorsement, repudiated the top of the Republican ticket and supported Vice President Humphrey, as did Mrs. Chisholm. Mr. Farmer had sought to encourage ticket-splitting by handing out leaflets urging "Vote Farmer First."

The Koch-Seymour race in the East Side's 17th Congressional District — produced few major disagreements between the two top candidates seeking to succeed Representative Theodore R. Kupferman, a Republican who did not seek re-election.

Both Mr. Koch and Mr. Seymour favored a halt in the bombing of North Vietnam. Both strongly advocated equal opportunities for Negroes. Mr. Koch, a 43-year-old bachelor, gained political prominence by defeating Carmine G. De Sapio, the former powerful New York County Democratic leader, three times, in 1963, 1964 and 1965, for the party's district leadership in Greenwich Village.

Mr. Seymour, a 44-year-old lawyer and member of an affluent New York family, is a former assistant United States Attorney and had been in the State Senate since 1965.

Reassessing Women's Political Role: The Lasting Impact of Geraldine Ferraro

BY MAUREEN DOWD | DEC. 30, 1984

WOMEN LOOKED AT HER and saw themselves, in a glass reflecting pride and prejudice, power and fear of power. As it turned out, her candidacy forced American women to grapple with their ambivalence about their own sex.

No one knew what Geraldine A. Ferraro was supposed to be. She did not remind you of anyone who had aspired to the inner sanctum. So every time she spoke, you had to make up your mind all over again whether she was good enough, tough enough, smart enough, honest enough to be the archetype. The profound question of whether she should be there at all was expressed in more trivial concerns. Her staccato style and her appearance became ways to gauge her worthiness. There was no reassuring masculine voice. There was no navy blue suit so redolent of power it seemed invisible. There were, instead, skirts flying in the wind, pocketbooks clutched at news conferences. And you caught yourself thinking incongruously: A Vice President with a purse? A Vice President whose favorite expression is "Gimme a break!"

Coming at a time of rapidly shifting ideas about the role of women in society and in the family, Geraldine Ferraro's candidacy evoked groping and contradictory perceptions among women — tribal pride and darker feelings of inferiority and jealousy.

The impact of the election will be felt for years. The way these women thought about Representative Ferraro and the way they voted has, in turn, forced feminists to reassess their role in politics and their future relationship with ordinary American women. It is also recasting the way the parties will deal with women — as voters, as candidates and as a movement.

Last summer, scores of women across the country said they were excited about the Ferraro nomination when they were called for a New York Times/CBS News poll. In new interviews, they have charted the course of their reactions to the historic race.

Theda Pate recalled the night she saw Geraldine Ferraro debate George Bush on television. "She hardly even blinked," Mrs. Pate marveled. "I thought, 'Wow, does she have some 200 I.Q. or something?' "

Then, as the elementary-school teacher from Pineville, La., watched the Representative from New York, she felt a spurt of envy tarring her approval. "She's not that much older than me," said Mrs. Pate, who is 42. "I don't think she's brilliant. Well read, maybe. And I thought maybe I could have been that if I had wanted to be. How do you know if you could have been, if you limited yourself in the very beginning? And she's attractive, no Margaret Mead or Eleanor Roosevelt. So I didn't have to think if I looked like them, I'd have to develop my mind, too.

"There's a type of subconscious envy, or maybe mistrust, of a woman who has succeeded where many others have not," she continued. "So instead of aggressively working to help her reach a position of prominence, we begin at an elementary level to attack. It's a basic flaw in women's behavior, which is to be bitchy."

In Bristol, Tenn., Carol Roberts said that she and her friends decided they were "maybe just a little afraid to leave ourselves in her hands if something was to happen."

"I put myself in her shoes," said the 36-year-old homemaker and mother of three. "Could I sit down and logically make decisions for everybody without cracking up? I think women in general are weak. I know that sounds awful. But we women know we have our faults. We look at ourselves and think 'I couldn't handle it so I don't know if she could, either.'

"Maybe that's the wrong thing to do," she said, in her soft Southern voice. "Men don't do that."

Mrs. Roberts and her husband, a postal clerk, voted for Ronald

Reagan. But she says that Mrs. Ferraro has made her feel different about women running for high office and about herself.

"She built us up a little. She said, 'Here's what you can do if you really want to do it. You don't have to sit at home and be a good housewife and mother — all that used to be required to make your niche.' She really kept herself together. She never broke down once. I'm proud she had the nerve to do what she did."

THE EUPHORIA DISSOLVES

Tracing the arc of a campaign bright with history and dark with disclosure, sorting through all the euphoria and champagne and tears, the analysts attempted after the election to calculate Geraldine Ferraro's worth to the Democratic ticket.

They drained all the history and emotion into dry statistics and, at The New York Times, reckoned that the first woman to run for the Vice Presidency on a major party ticket represented a net gain of eight-tenths of 1 percentage point. The fraction mocked the memory of the Democratic convention in San Francisco last July, when her selection seemed suddenly to transform the image of the party from one of stale egalitarianism into one of possibility.

As I go over my notes from the Democratic convention, it is possible to re-create the aura that led so many Democrats to envision a shining year for women in politics, a year when Geraldine Ferraro would unleash "small-f" feminism — that flickering and apolitical sense of injustice they felt was common to all American women. The mood was so electric that just being female felt terrific. "One man I know told me I even looked stronger," said Jane O'Reilly, a New York writer floating through the crowd. Democratic women challenging incumbents for Congressional seats were suddenly the stars of fund-raising rallies, and they bubbled with talk of how the Ferraro choice would bring money, volunteers and credibility to their campaigns.

None of these particular women, whose elation filled my notebooks, were elected. "It turned into the biggest non-event in history," scoffed

Robert Dole, the Senate's new majority leader, discussing "The Year of the Woman."

The feminists who promised Walter F. Mondale an outpouring of votes and volunteers have been despondent, scrambling to explain why a majority of American women preferred the President some feminists call "the Caveman."

Some political bosses in districts where women ran and lost have been grumbling privately about women making bad candidates. Some Democratic leaders are talking publicly about the party's need to distance itself from special interest groups, like women. And memos have circulated among Republican politicians about the "antifemale backlash" in the vote.

In the end, ironically, the election was dominated by the fight for the white male vote and played out in the rhetoric and imagery of machismo. After Geraldine Ferraro was chosen, Democratic Senator Lloyd Bentsen of Texas joked that he would probably be the last white Anglo-Saxon male to be considered for the Vice Presidency. Now, drumbeats sound in Democratic circles that, for jobs like national party chairman, a white Anglo-Saxon male would be best.

"We can't afford to have a party so feminized that it has no appeal to males," said Patrick Caddell, the Democratic consultant.

HOW WOMEN VOTED

"I think we can declare the gender gap closed," said Elizabeth Hanford Dole, President Reagan's Secretary of Transportation.

Not quite. While it disappeared nationally in the Reagan landslide, the gender gap did affect Republican losses in the Senate, where it showed up as a significant factor in races in Michigan, Illinois and Massachusetts. It also helped Madeleine M. Kunin to become the first female Governor of Vermont.

The women's groups have lost some political clout because they did not deliver their sisters. But most analysts now say that the vote was simply not there to be delivered.

"The idea that Geraldine Ferraro or women controlled the women's vote is as crazy as the A.F.L.-C.I.O. delivering labor's vote," said William Schneider, a political analyst. "Votes are no longer deliverable in this day and age."

One thing the year did prove is that the women's vote does not respond simply to the symbol of a woman's candidacy.

"There has always been an ambiguous relationship of women voting for women candidates," said Ethel Klein, an associate professor at Columbia University and the author of the book "Gender Politics." "Unlike blacks and other minorities, women do not vote on self-interest. They vote for a better society as a whole. Women see as selfish the argument of 'Vote for someone because she's a woman like you and you'll personally gain.' "

There was also a lingering feeling that Geraldine Ferraro's sex superseded her qualifications. "We put a woman on the ticket who would not have been on the ticket unless she was a woman," said Patrick Caddell. "And even though Geraldine Ferraro did terrifically, there was a sense that Mondale was forced into taking a woman by the women's groups."

Women voters were most happy with Mrs. Ferraro in the first few days, before her halo slipped. "Women are generally more inclined to support women candidates unless there's a problem," said Kathy Wilson, president of the National Women's Political Caucus. "Then, women candidates don't resuscitate themselves as quickly. The financial thing was a problem for Ferraro with women. It destroyed her momentum. And it shook the Mondale campaign's confidence in their ability to use her."

The flap about her family's finances muddied Mrs. Ferraro's fresh image and robbed her of a getting-to-know-you phase she dearly needed.

"I didn't even know a Geraldine Ferraro existed until I heard her name announced," said Tamara Fish, a freshman at Harvard College. "I ran to the library and tried to find information on this Geraldine

Ferraro. It seemed a bit awkward to pick a running mate no one knows anything about out of the blue," said the 18-year-old from Cleveland. "You should know who it is before the deadline. Mondale not only introduced her to the entire country but then expected to win their support. It takes more than a few months to get a sense for someone."

Feminists have argued strongly that it would have been possible to elicit a women's vote if the Mondale-Ferraro campaign had spent more time wooing it with a revolutionary strategy designed to exploit the Vice Presidential candidate's historic status. "In this particular election, women were ignored," said Marlene Johnson, Lieutenant Governor of Minnesota, who was one of the most persuasive voices last summer in convincing Mr. Mondale to choose a woman. While her remark sounds incredible under the circumstances, it is significant because it shows the extent of the hard feelings among feminists toward the Mondale campaign strategists.

"There's a new family situation in this country," she explained. "Almost 50 percent of children under 6 live in families where women work and more families are headed by women. They don't always have resources for child care, or to see that their children get educated properly or live in safe neighborhoods with decent housing. We didn't talk about that in this campaign."

Lieutenant Governor Johnson and Dotty Lynch, a polltaker who did some work for Mr. Mondale, argued that he and Mrs. Ferraro should have been seen together more often in campaign stops and advertisements as an eloquent promise of a new era in which men and women share power.

But Mr. Mondale's inner circle of "smart-ass white boys," as they were dubbed by many blacks and feminists in the party, cast Mrs. Ferraro in the role of a traditional running mate, part hatchet man, part echo chamber.

"If you want my frank opinion, after they named Ferraro, they got scared," said Betty Friedan. "They got so worried about the white male backlash, they didn't want us women doing what we did before."

Amid increasing tension with the Mondale men, women's groups tried to mobilize the troops, but, with campaign funds pouring into the media and polls rather than into grass-roots organizing, the groups could scarcely find what they now scathingly call "the phantom campaign."

"Women called in all over the state and expected to be put to work," said Linda Davidoff, the chairman of Women for Mondale-Ferraro in New York. "And then they found out to their frustration — we must've gotten the comment 500 times — nothing is happening out here."

Referring to the feminists' complaints that Mrs. Ferraro should have been seen more in commercials and shows on daytime television, Francis J. O'Brien, the candidate's iconoclastic press aide, replied acidly: "What did they want us to do, 'As the World Turns'?"

THE NEXT TIME

It has become a favorite parlor game among the political cognoscenti to debate whether Mrs. Ferraro's candidacy will make it more or less likely that a woman will be on a national ticket in 1988.

"I think we see dynamics at work where it may lead to the Vice Presidential spot being 'the woman's spot,' " said Lee Atwater, a Reagan-Bush strategist.

Taking a page from Jesse Jackson's campaign, a woman may end up running on her own in the Democratic primaries, but the odds are that the Democrats will not choose one for the second spot next time, largely because they need to focus on recouping the blue-collar white males they have been losing since 1968.

The Republicans, on the other hand, could keep their strong base of white males and expand into the two areas they need to solidify — women and "yuppies" — by choosing a woman. As William Schneider said wryly, "The ideal Republican candidate is a woman. The ideal Democratic candidate is a general."

Even Republicans who think Mrs. Ferraro hurt the Democrats blame it on her personal drawbacks — her liberalism, the financial controversy, her "strident" style — rather than her sex. They think their pool of high-ranking women erases any public perception of tokenism and that a coed ticket could do wonders for the G.O.P. in a year when a bitter primary race is expected.

"Kemp and Kirkpatrick," said George L. Clark Jr., the head of the New York State Republican Party, his voice hushed with reverence, as he referred to Representative Jack F. Kemp and Jeane J. Kirkpatrick, United States chief delegate to the United Nations. "I've heard that one more times than the hair on my head. And I have a lot of hair on my head."

One pundit joked that another Presidential contender, Senator Dole, will soon have to ask his wife, the Transportation Secretary, whether she prefers the title of First Lady or Vice President.

"I'm sure Bush and Baker are devising a strategy right now that would cut me off by having a woman on the ticket," said Mr. Dole, referring to the political plans of Vice President George Bush and Senator Howard H. Baker Jr.

And doesn't that make life a little awkward since he is living with the woman they might be thinking of?

"I kid her about it a lot," he said. "I say, 'Boy, it sounds like a great opportunity.' But it doesn't seem to ring any bells with her. Unless she's cagier than I think she is."

Certainly, the Ferraro experience will affect the sort of woman who is chosen next time, and the method of that choice. There will be no more blind dates with history. "We should try to choose someone who already has a national image," said Gloria Steinem.

THE CANDIDATE REMEMBERS

Circumscribed by campaign etiquette, they did not begin their historic relationship with a kiss. But they ended it with one.

"When I spoke to Fritz on the phone on Election Day," Mrs. Ferraro recalls, "I said, 'When I see you, I'm going to give you a kiss and I don't care who's standing there, because I think you're terrific!'" Their rendezvous took place in a cold airport office in Washington, where their planes touched down the day after the election.

"Fritz is a good friend and he deserves a lot of credit," she said. "I'm sure there were times when he must have thought, 'What did I do this for?' But that was never conveyed to me."

Representative Ferraro is back in her Queens district office on a darkening December afternoon, alone now except for her longtime aide Pat Flynn and two secretaries.

She is asked if the First Woman had to be perfect.

"Yeah. Probably. I wasn't."

She feels that the body blows she experienced in the campaign will make it easier for the next woman.

"Next time around you're going to find women running in the primaries. I think that's where you're going to have the opportunity to be tested. The decision about whether or not she wants to do it is not going to be something that's done in 48 hours. She's going to look at my candidacy and, especially if she's married, say to her husband, 'Let's sit down and go through everything. And I mean everything. Let's pretend you live in a police state and you're going to have them check you out.' "

Mrs. Ferraro spends her days mulling offers from Manhattan law firms, debating whether to run for the Senate and working on a campaign memoir that will help pay off, among other things, $51,000 in accountants' bills. She plans to be frank but not nasty in the book, the rights to which she has just sold for about $1 million. "I'm really not a word that rhymes with rich," she says, with a fey grin.

She doesn't regret losing her Congressional seat. "The public works committee is interesting, but if you've heard enough testimony on coal slurry pipelines, you kind of figure out that there must be something better in life," she says.

Tanned and relaxed from a St. Croix vacation, she wears dangling gold earrings bearing her monogram and a purple knit dress with Joan Crawford shoulders. "These are my favorite earrings and I never wore them during the whole campaign," she says, fingering them reflectively. "They're too gypsyish. I had to go to a lot of conservative areas in the South and elsewhere."

Now she wears what she likes. And, free of nervous aides who tried to tone down her tendency to be "flip lipped," she says what she likes.

The day before the election, when it was clear that the Democrats were going to lose badly, Geraldine Ferraro and Maryland Representative Barbara A. Mikulski reflected on whether her candidacy had had the right stuff.

"Barbara said, 'Gerry, it's kind of like breaking the sound barrier for the first time.' You know, those guys in those planes starting to get to Mach 1 and Mach 2, or whatever it is they do to break the barrier. We got shaken up and pushed and pulled in a lot of directions. We didn't do it, but it's only the first time."

Campaign aides maintain that Mrs. Ferraro was the best choice. "If you lose 49 states, where was she a drag — Delaware?" says Francis O'Brien.

As Mrs. Ferraro sees it, "I thought I would do a little bit better with women." It is odd, she adds, how analysts say women were too sophisticated to vote for a woman, and yet argue that Southerners would not have been too sophisticated to vote for Lloyd Bentsen.

In a race that often seemed a qualifying test of toughness, with reporters waiting to pounce on the first trace of a tear, Mrs. Ferraro's grit never faltered. She prided herself on not getting nervous, but she concedes she was scared before she debated George Bush.

"If I had said anything dumb, I really felt that would be making a mistake for every woman sitting out there," she said.

Mrs. Ferraro has just returned from lunch with her cousin Nicholas Ferraro, the former District Attorney of Queens County who launched her political career by hiring her as a prosecutor in his office. He told her she had erred during the debate when she told the Vice President not to patronize her. "Men don't like to hear that," he chastised gently. "If I weren't on national TV, I probably would have turned around and said 'Gimme a break!' " she said.

She plays the "If she were a he" game about Mr. Bush. "Suppose I had gushed about Gromyko? Suppose I had said, 'Would you rather talk about the World Series?' If I had acted as jumpy and giddy as he did, they would have destroyed me."

Referring to critics who said she had faltered on foreign affairs, she asked sarcastically, "If I can't discuss arms control and war and peace because I've never been in a war, why should these guys be allowed to discuss abortion?"

Beyond the debate, there were other pressures. Mrs. Ferraro led an odd double life, campaigning brightly and tirelessly even as the published reports mounted about investigations into the financial affairs of her husband, John A. Zaccaro, and about speculation on ties to organized crime.

"We used to get up every morning and look at the headlines. I'd get up and say 'What's in it today?' John and I literally did not sleep. But I sure as heck wasn't going to let anybody know that I was down."

Now, she does come close to tears when talking about some of the charges, and there are flashes of bitterness. She believes, based on information that she has received from "friends in criminal justice," that the Republicans leaked information on her family through Federal law-enforcement agencies to blacken her candidacy, a charge a spokesman for the Reagan-Bush campaign dismissed as a "ridiculous thought."

"Whatever they did to me is one thing," Mrs. Ferraro said, "but going after my husband and my father on stuff from 40, 50 years ago? I've never seen anything done like this to anybody. Take Ronald Reagan. How many people know that his father was an alcoholic? Do any of us care?"

There was constant speculation about the ravages of the race on Mrs. Ferraro's marriage.

Clearly, Geraldine Ferraro and John Zaccaro know a lot more about each other than they did five months ago. A friend recalled the moment, at a meeting with accountants preparing for her marathon financial disclosure press conference, when Mrs. Ferraro discovered that her husband had set up an extra trust fund for their son.

Giving her husband a steely glance, she said, "My two daughters will each have an extra trust fund on Monday morning."

At a party in Los Angeles, Frank Sinatra remarked, according to a top Reagan aide, that he reckoned "when this is all over, Zaccaro is going to divorce that broad." In a beauty parlor at a Phoenix resort recently, the manager told patrons that Mrs. Ferraro had filed for divorce.

She has grown accustomed to the buzz about "splitsville," as she calls it. "People are saying I would walk out on him because of this stuff. I said if that man doesn't leave me after what he's been subjected to, he deserves sainthood." She talked of a second honeymoon this summer to the Far East to celebrate their 25th anniversary.

She is asked if the campaign was worth the public dissection and replies it will depend on whether her husband comes safely out of the investigations. "If we get through it, and he's all right, I guess we will both say yeah, it was worth it."

THE FEMINISTS' FUTURE

The message the election sent to the women's movement varies widely, depending on who's talking. Most analysts agree with Mr. Schneider that the message is: "Don't try and push politicians around. Demanding concessions from politicians is the way to ruin your own image and the image of the Democratic Party."

But many feminists agree with Laura D. Blackburn, an attorney and president of the Institute for Mediation and Conflict Resolution, who deduced quite a different message recently after a meeting of the National Organization for Women: "I think we can stop asking now and demand — not just let the smart-ass white boys make the decisions about campaigns."

Gloria Steinem suggested a more independent route. "All signs indicate we have to stop wasting so much time convincing Democratic Party leaders and do our own homework and elect our own candidates," she said.

Although most women's leaders feel "chastened," as Dotty Lynch put it, they are already plotting strategies. They want to move away from the practice of putting women into "scapegoat" races against tough incumbents and look for more vulnerable seats. They plan to recruit women legislators aggressively, as well as business and cultural leaders, to get more candidates into the pipeline. "We have to think ahead a dozen years instead of one," said Gloria Steinem.

A few days after Harriett Woods, a Democrat, was elected Lieutenant Governor of Missouri last month, a group of women, unbeknownst to her, got together in a private meeting in Washington to begin planning her Senate campaign for 1986. Two years ago, she lost a Senate race to John C. Danforth by less than two points, after squeezing money out of a national party which was skeptical that a woman could win. Now, she is sanguine about the election results and talks about improvements in the political mood. "The fact that I was the first woman elected statewide in Missouri did not even make the headlines this time," she says.

Many analysts claimed that the elections showed that the feminists are out of touch with average American women.

"The women's movement needs to make being a housewife and mother very much more acceptable," said Edith P. Mayo, a curator in the division of political history at the Smithsonian Institution.

It is a sensitive issue, but some feminists admit they must "repackage" their rhetoric and issues.

"We need to have patience with our sisters and we need to understand that our perspectives are determined by the Washington political environment," said Joanne Symons, director of political education for the American Nurses' Association. "A great deal of education still needs to occur."

FERRARO'S LEGACY

In the end, Mrs. Ferraro probably made no difference in the outcome of the 1984 Presidential race.

And, while that leaves a sour taste now for feminists, because it sometimes seemed as though the political fate of American women rested on the 1984 election, it will be interpreted differently in the history books.

"It was all fairly predictable and in the normal mode of American politics," said Mr. Schneider. "And isn't that what women want? Can you imagine nominating a black and saying it made no difference?"

Mrs. Ferraro's legacy is best measured in shattered stereotypes. If male politicians whistle "Hail to the Chief" when they shave in the morning, jokes Michael Barone, a Washington opinion analyst, women can now whistle it as they brush their hair.

Putting a woman on the ticket did evoke a backlash of sexist sentiment and crude jokes.

"I talked to men on the road," reported Anne Wexler, a Ferraro adviser, "who said, 'I'm not voting for her because she belongs in the home, she belongs back with her kids, what the hell is she doing this for?'"

Rich Bond, a Republican consultant and former aide to George Bush, added that the climate was ripe for machismo. "There was no Machiavellian strategy behind Bush's locker room comment after the debate," said Mr. Bond. "But it worked fine. It did him a lot of good with Johnny Lunchbucket and Johnny Sixpack out there saying 'Goddamn right, kick a little ass!'"

The women are pragmatic, however. They agree that the reaction among men represents a necessary catharsis and they give the candidate credit for having taken the brunt of that reaction.

Mrs. Ferraro's contribution will also be measured in the way women think about themselves and leadership. "That vision of that woman and the Vice President of the United States standing toe-to-toe is implanted in female brains all across this country, and it will germinate in a lot of different ways," said Joanne Symons. "Whenever a woman goes in to ask her boss for a raise, she'll have a sense of 'I have a right to stand here. Don't patronize me, Mr. Bush.'"

Ann Richards, the State Treasurer of Texas, agreed: "How do you translate what happened to that little girl in the third grade who saw a woman running for Vice President? We'll only know by the speeches she makes when she's 25 and running for office that it made a difference in her life."

And, certainly, Mrs. Ferraro's legacy will last forever in the hearts of such women as Georgene Goetting, known to her friends as just George.

At her bridge club, at weddings, at the grocery store on double-coupon day, George listened to women sing Mrs. Ferraro's faults. "Those women don't have much faith in themselves," sniffed the amiable 63-year-old, who lives with her husband, Ralph, a retired Culligan soft-water man, in Beaver Dam, Wis.

She sent Mrs. Ferraro a check for $100, the first campaign contribution she had ever made. And she planted a large Mondale-Ferraro sign in her yard.

"Women have come a long way and we have such a long way to go yet," she said. "I couldn't find a thing to fault her on. She is kind of a heroine, if I'm looking for one."

The day after the election, George tied a black velvet ribbon around the campaign sign in her yard. When she came home that evening, she was surprised to find both gone. The woman scorned had become a hot collector's item. "It made me feel rather good," said George, with a twinkle. "At least my granddaughters will know I was so much for her, so enthused by her candidacy. And they'll know I believed we would move forward."

To Understand Clinton's Moment, Consider That It Came 32 Years After Ferraro's

BY ALISON MITCHELL | JUNE 11, 2016

THE SCENES BLEND like images from a kaleidoscope. A woman, blond, jubilant in a white dress, shown magnified on a convention center screen in San Francisco. It is Geraldine A. Ferraro in 1984 accepting the Democratic nomination that made her the first woman in the nation to be tapped by a major party to run for vice president.

Turn the lens. A woman, blond, in a white tunic, smiling, arms thrown wide at a rally in Brooklyn this past week. It is Hillary Clinton claiming the Democratic nomination, the first woman to become the presidential standard-bearer for a major party.

There are those who now say that a woman running for president was inevitable, that the 18 million cracks in the glass ceiling that Mrs. Clinton talks about are just time moving on. There are the sighs that Mrs. Clinton is the wrong woman, the unexciting woman, the compromising woman. And there are those who say they could never vote for a Democrat, particularly this one.

But it took 32 years to get from one scene to the other, so a look back to the Ferraro campaign can tell a lot about how the country has changed, and how it has not, through these decades of cultural ferment over the roles of the sexes.

It may be hard to remember how few women there were in public life when Ms. Ferraro told cheering Democrats, "If we can do this, we can do anything." The Democrats had no female senators. (The Republicans had two.) There was only one female governor — Martha Layne Collins of Kentucky, a Democrat. Dianne Feinstein was still the mayor of San Francisco, yet to start her long Senate career. Representative Shirley Chisholm of New York, who unsuccessfully sought the Democratic nomination in 1972, had already retired.

Women have since become the majority in college, and women in both parties have made a steady march forward in politics. Some are senators and governors and three have been secretary of state, all making the idea of a woman at the helm of the nation seem far less revolutionary.

Ms. Ferraro was quizzed relentlessly about arms control and about whether she could even be credible as the commander in chief should she have to step up and be president. Could a woman be trusted with the nuclear button?

But with her background as secretary of state, Mrs. Clinton is not questioned about her toughness. Instead, the left asks whether she might be too quick to seek military intervention and the right critiques her judgment. She is the one now asking whether Donald J. Trump's finger should be anywhere near the nuclear button.

In other ways, things have changed less. As Mrs. Clinton, Sarah Palin and Carly Fiorina can attest, female candidates are still examined not only for competence, character and policy priorities, but for the way they look, the tone of their voice and the state of their marriages.

For Ms. Ferraro it was the tangled financial dealings of her husband, John Zaccaro, his subsidy of her first congressional campaign, and her back and forth on whether she would release his tax returns, which she tried to brush off with the damaging quip, "You people who are married to Italian men, you know what it's like."

Now Mr. Trump promises to keep the Clinton marriage, and the former president's infamous infidelities, in the spotlight. Mrs. Clinton time and again had to help save her husband's candidacy and presidency, tarnishing her feminist credentials for some. ("I'm not sitting here — some little woman standing by my man like Tammy Wynette," she said way back in 1992, when his run for president nearly foundered. "I'm sitting here because I love him, and I respect him, and I honor what he's been through and what we've been through together.")

SARA KRULWICH/THE NEW YORK TIMES

Geraldine Ferraro and Walter F. Mondale, the Democratic nominee for president, in 1984.

And then there is the press corps. Politico recently wrote of the current crop of Clinton reporters, "No one can remember a political press corps this heavily female."

I can. It was the Ferraro press corps, and I was part of it. I was dispatched to the campaign — like women from most major networks and publications — because editors sought women to capture the history of one of their own at a time when we were breaking into the ranks of the campaign press. Perhaps, we occasionally suspected, some of them also thought it would be beneath a man to ride that campaign plane.

As a reporter for Newsday, I watched the euphoric, rapturous crowds, mostly women and girls who showed up with "To Gerry with Love" signs, even in the campaign's last days, when it was going down to a decisive defeat to President Reagan and George Bush. Some campaign bands could make you wince, playing "Five Foot Two, Eyes of Blue" or "Hello, Dolly!"

SARA KRULWICH/THE NEW YORK TIMES

Ms. Ferraro on "Meet the Press," with Roger Mudd, left, and Marvin Kalb, in October 1984. She was once asked on the program, "Do you think that in any way the Soviets might be tempted to try to take advantage of you simply because you are a woman?"

There were the strange male missteps: the mayor of Los Angeles saying he wanted "a vice president I can hug," the Mississippi official who called Ms. Ferraro "young lady" and asked whether she could bake a blueberry muffin. The grim drumbeat about her husband's finances, his real estate dealings and his tax returns. There was the constant watch for weakness — would the woman cry?

It is easy to forget those moments these days, when women in power don't seem so unusual. If you have a long memory you have watched other women on the national stage, too. Representative Patricia Schroeder explored a Democratic race in 1987, after Gary Hart stood down. Senator Elizabeth Dole dropped out of the Republican presidential race in October 1999 before any of the primaries. Former Senator Carol Moseley Braun ran in the Democratic primaries in 2004. Governor Palin of Alaska became the first Republican woman nominated for the vice presidency in 2008 — 24 years after Ms. Ferraro. And we have been watching Mrs. Clinton for so long, through so many iterations, that it can feel like we know everything about her.

But in the 1980s the quest to put a woman in the White House started as a cause without a candidate. It was driven by women's groups and by the numbers. The notion of a gender gap was being talked about by both parties. Suddenly it was significant that more women than men registered to vote and that women seemed more likely to vote.

The Equal Rights Amendment had collapsed, failing to win the required ratification of three-fourths of the states. Politically active women in the feminist movement, including Bella Abzug and Gloria Steinem, wrote a manifesto to the Democratic candidates for president in 1983 warning them to agree on an agenda for issues affecting women or face the possibility of women staying home on Election Day: "We will not hold still to be treated as an afterthought, a side issue, or a powerless constituency that can be betrayed without consequences." By 1984, they were fighting to get a woman on the ticket.

When Walter F. Mondale selected Ms. Ferraro as his running mate, she was a three-term congresswoman from Queens. She came from New York, which had unexpectedly swung to Ronald Reagan in his 1980 landslide. Speaker Thomas P. O'Neill Jr. was a mentor and proponent. She was pretty, married, 48 years old and traditional enough that party leaders thought she could excite women but might not alienate male voters.

"What is different," says Ann Lewis, a longtime Democratic activist, "is that Hillary Clinton in the last 20-25 years has achieved national stature in ways that too few women have. Gerry Ferraro is nominated in 1984 and she is almost unknown. It isn't until 1986 that Barbara Mikulski becomes the first Democratic woman who makes it to the Senate in her own right."

The mood at that convention was electric. But the choreography around this first woman could also be tortured. How should Mr. Mondale and Ms. Ferraro share the stage? Could they touch? They shouldn't hug. Who should hold her pocketbook when she spoke? "It sounds so strange now, but everything was being done for the first time," Ms. Lewis said. "We had until then lots of images of women and men on stage together, but they were married. All the stage craft we had taken for granted had to be looked at very carefully."

Madeleine K. Albright was Ms. Ferraro's issues adviser, briefing the candidate on foreign policy and preparing her for her race against Mr. Bush, years before Ms. Albright became the nation's first female secretary of state in the Clinton administration. She remembers some of the jarring juxtapositions of that candidacy. "There was the business about what she had on and what her hair looked like," she recalls. "On the other side was her being asked questions about throw weights and nuclear capabilities that they weren't asking Bush."

On "Meet the Press," Ms. Ferraro was once asked, "Do you think that in any way the Soviets might be tempted to try to take advantage of you simply because you are a woman?"

By November, the disclosures about Ms. Ferraro's husband's businesses had damaged a campaign that was already an uphill battle. Though women and girls showed up at her rallies to the end, TV network polls showed that she may have cost the Democratic ticket more than she gained for it.

Looking back, was the scrutiny of Ms. Ferraro, who died in 2011, fair game or driven by discomfort with the idea of a woman as vice president? Ms. Ferraro's campaign manager, John Sasso, calls it some of both. "Experience matters," he said, noting that because Mrs. Clinton has the deep résumé that Ms. Ferraro lacked, she will run and face a very different campaign.

This time, of course, the first woman is at the top of the ticket, calling all the shots.

"She's been on the front lines of this process for a very long time," said Lissa Muscatine, a friend and former speechwriter to Mrs. Clinton. "She's been the vessel for lots of women's hopes on the one hand, but also has had to take the brunt from people who aren't ready for it."

Mrs. Clinton's detractors look dimly on appeals to support her as a pathbreaker. "I'm not a huge fan of identity politics and this is sort of the apotheosis of identity politics," said Danielle Pletka, senior vice president for foreign and defense policy studies at the conservative American Enterprise Institute. "Basically, to me Hillary Clinton is saying: 'I wasn't good enough to get here on my own. Forget that people voted for me on the merits, they voted for me because I was a woman.' How demeaning is that?" On Friday, Ms. Fiorina, who ran for the Republican presidential nomination this year, told a crowd, "Hillary Clinton, news flash. I'm a feminist and I'm not voting for you."

Maybe Hillary Clinton is right — that she has become our national Rorschach test. Do you admire her perseverance? Dislike her compromises? Seek more passion? Question her honesty? Ponder her marriage? Love her policies? Hate her policies? Debate whether she is a feminist? Debate whether it matters? For one night last week, it was hard to deny her words that "tonight caps an amazing journey — a long, long journey."

Hillary Clinton Ignited a Feminist Movement. By Losing.

BY AMY CHOZICK | JAN. 13, 2018

HILLARY CLINTON, the first woman who had a real shot at the presidency, has finally set off a national awakening among women. The only catch? She did it by losing.

In the year since a stoic Mrs. Clinton watched as Donald J. Trump was sworn in as the 45th president, a fervor has swept the country, prompting women's marches, a record number of female candidates running for office and an outcry about sexual assault at all levels of society.

Even those women who disliked Hillary-the-candidate or who backed her opponent Senator Bernie Sanders in the Democratic primary now credit the indignities and cynicism Mrs. Clinton faced in the 2016 election and her unexpected loss to Mr. Trump, an alleged sexual abuser, for the current moment.

We wouldn't be here — black gowns at the Golden Globes, sexual assault victims invited to the State of the Union address, a nationwide, woman-led voter registration drive timed to the anniversary of the Women's March — without Mrs. Clinton's defeat.

And yet, for Mrs. Clinton, it's the latest — and perhaps last — cruel twist in a public life full of them. Her loss to Mr. Trump helped ignite the kind of movement she'd once been poised to lead but that she now mostly watches from the sidelines.

Ever since she wielded a bullhorn at Wellesley in the late 1960s and later instructed her classmates to "practice politics as the art of making what appears to be impossible possible," Hillary Rodham seemed destined to empower women. But over the next several decades, the promise of that young activist collided with the realities of presidential elections and her husband's personal scandals.

Mrs. Clinton — scarred by the blowback for saying she chose to pursue a career rather than staying home to bake cookies, chastised by her husband's West Wing aides for declaring that "women's rights are human rights" in Beijing in 1995 and warned by her 2016 campaign chairman to avoid talking about glass ceilings — came to adopt a more tentative embrace of how she talked about her gender.

Throughout her career, many women would view Mrs. Clinton as an imperfect vessel for the feminist cause. She was a Yale-educated lawyer who at the height of the 1970s women's movement moved to Arkansas to put her own ambitions on hold in furtherance of her husband's career. A refrain I'd often hear from voters on the 2016 campaign trail was that they were happy to vote for a woman, just not "that woman."

But the roiling, messy, often painful progress made since Mr. Trump took office has recast Mrs. Clinton, who recently topped Gallup's poll of most admired women. Her career brings to light the truth that there is no perfect vessel, that sooner or later, the harder we strive, the higher we climb, we all become that woman.

It's now nearly a year since several million women with pink pussy hats and homemade signs took to the streets in cities across the country to protest Mr. Trump. Mrs. Clinton didn't attend the Women's March on Washington, but the role she played in spurring the current wave of activism has become more clear.

"None of us were prepared for this loss in the sense that we didn't have well-laid plans to mobilize," said Cecile Richards, president of Planned Parenthood. "But that's what's happened, it's been a year of channeling, catching up to the activism as much as trying to foment engagement."

After Mr. Trump's victory, the concerns that women would be reluctant to come forward with accusations of sexual assault and harassment spread, given that millions of Americans and a majority of white female voters seemed unfazed by an audio recording of Mr. Trump bragging about violating women.

"To watch him win was to make women feel like 'I just exposed myself for absolutely nothing,' " said Joan Walsh, a writer for The Nation and a CNN political analyst.

But the opposite happened. The collective voice of victims of sexual assault, spurred by the revelations against the movie producer Harvey Weinstein and other powerful men, has become a forceful, cathartic revolt.

Political analysts predicted that Mrs. Clinton's loss would cause women to retreat from running for public office, turned off by the combat and nastiness ushered in by a reality-TV star who vanquished the bookish, dutiful woman. Instead, data shows the number of women seeking office is rising at every level.

In her recent book, "What Happened," Mrs. Clinton is forthright about the country's mixed opinions of her and about the news media's treatment of her (including by Matt Lauer, who has since been fired from NBC News after he was accused of inappropriate sexual behavior). "Then there was the matter of my gender," Mrs. Clinton writes.

But on issues of sexual assault, Mrs. Clinton has remained mostly muted, her hands tied as liberals rethink how President Bill Clinton's accusers were dismissed and shamed in the 1990s. Even the #StillWithHer crowd seems to agree that the #MeToo movement cannot feature Mrs. Clinton.

In November, Patti Solis Doyle, a senior aide to Mrs. Clinton from 1991 to 2008, published an article on CNN's website in which she said she didn't take the allegations of sexual harassment and assault against Mr. Clinton as seriously as she should have.

In an interview, Ms. Solis Doyle said that she and other White House aides considered quitting at the time but that would have just hurt Mrs. Clinton. "Why would we punish her for his actions?" Even so, Ms. Solis Doyle said that, as for Mrs. Clinton, the #MeToo movement "is one area she cannot go."

In the days after several Hollywood actresses told The Times and The New Yorker that Mr. Weinstein, a longtime donor to the Clintons, had harassed or assaulted them, Mrs. Clinton denounced his behavior, saying she was "shocked and appalled by the revelations."

A debate ensued, with feminists asking why Mrs. Clinton always seemed to be held responsible for the badly behaving men around her. "The people saying, 'Why won't Hillary go away?' are the same people saying, 'Why hasn't Hillary condemned this terrible thing that's happened,' " said Nita Chaudhary, a founder of UltraViolet, a women's advocacy group.

It's impossible to know whether the #MeToo movement would have swept the nation had Mrs. Clinton finally shattered "that highest, hardest glass ceiling."

Conservative critics argue that a second Clinton administration would have allowed Mr. Weinstein to maintain his status as Hollywood kingmaker and powerful Democratic donor. "The predators, most of them media and Hollywood liberals, would still be in power," Michael Goodwin wrote in a column in The New York Post that Mr. Trump recommended to his 46.6 million Twitter followers.

Liberals say, policy advancements aside, Mrs. Clinton's victory would probably have led to a brief period of euphoria and a return to complacency — or worse, a backlash against ambitious women.

Mrs. Clinton enters a select club of losing presidential candidates whose defeats lead to larger cultural movements. In 1964, Barry Goldwater was defeated by Lyndon B. Johnson in a landslide, but the bruising finish motivated conservatives to organize, establish think tanks, publish right-leaning magazines and encourage other conservatives to run.

"It took a while, but eventually the movement surfaced with Ronald Reagan," said Doris Kearns Goodwin, the historian. "That was the success that came out of the huge failure of 1964."

Ms. Goodwin sees parallels to what Mrs. Clinton's loss to Mr. Trump (and in her case, winning of the popular vote) could lead to among women. "It's hard to see when you're in the middle of it," she said. "But it feels like something's happening, a fervor, an excitement, an optimism."

Even before Mr. Trump took the oath of office, some feminists sought to move beyond the Clinton years. Last January, the organizers of the Woman's March on Washington released a list of 28 "revolutionary leaders who paved the way for us to march," including Shirley Chisholm, Gloria Steinem and Malala Yousafzai. The list did not include Mrs. Clinton.

In October, the Women's March faced criticism for choosing Mr. Sanders to speak on the opening night of its national convention. (The organizers later apologized, and Mr. Sanders bowed out.)

Linda Sarsour, a co-founder of the Women's March who supported Mr. Sanders in the primary, credited Mr. Trump's victory — not Mrs. Clinton's defeat — with the current reckoning among women. "People were so aghast and felt betrayed that so many of our fellow Americans voted for a misogynist, accused sexual predator," she said.

The 2018 midterm elections will test whether the Women's March and related movements can translate into electoral power, the way conservatives eventually turned the 1964 rout into the Reagan revolution. In the meantime, allies of Mrs. Clinton see something tragic about the Trump era, and the resistance mounting against it, as the final note to her public life.

"I guess every cloud has its silver lining, and this is it," Ms. Solis Doyle said. "But in terms of Hillary's perspective and career it's sad that it comes as she's diminishing, some would say vanishing, from the political stage."

A Man Among Female Leaders: 'The Risk of Mansplaining Is Very High'

BY KATRIN BENNHOLD | DEC. 2, 2017

REYKJAVIK, ICELAND — Xavier Prats Monné could not say what exactly he expected from Iceland, this tiny gender utopia where selling pornography has been banned since 1869 and the world's first openly lesbian prime minister was elected in 2009. But it was no shock that the driver who picked him up from the airport was a woman.

Until she offered to help with his luggage.

"What? No, no, no, no, no," Mr. Prats Monné replied, alarmed, and hastily picked up his suitcase himself. "No, no, no. Thank you."

Mr. Prats Monné, 61, a quick-witted Spaniard with a ready laugh, runs the 900-employee department of health and food safety for the European Commission, the executive branch of the European Union. He routinely mingles with Europe ministers and, once, met President Barack Obama.

But this past week, he was in Iceland to speak at what was billed as the largest ever gathering of female political leaders, sponsored by a nonprofit devoted to increasing their numbers. Less than one-quarter of parliamentary seats worldwide are held by women. Among heads of state, 7 percent are female.

The summit meeting drew more than 300 current and former female lawmakers, prime ministers and presidents. At a time when scandals of sexual misconduct in the workplace are roiling society, Mr. Prats Monné was one of a few men on the roster of speakers.

His topic: maternal health.

"When you speak to an audience of women about motherhood and you are a man, the risk of mansplaining is very high," he admitted.

I had sought out Mr. Prats Monné because I was curious: At an international conference of politicians, how does a man feel when he is in the minority? What could it tell us about gender equality?

An anthropologist by training, Mr. Prats Monné was intrigued. "I deal with primates every day," he said of his male colleagues. "Maybe this will be different?"

He agreed to let me shadow him for 24 hours.

At 5.30 p.m., that female driver, a 27-year-old named Erla, was taking us to our first event: a reception hosted by Iceland's former president Vigdis Finnbogadottir, 87, whose cult status is such that all Icelanders refer to her by her first name. Vigdis means war goddess in Old Norse. In 1980, she became the country's (and the world's) first directly elected female president — and was a single mother to boot.

Erla told us that gender roles were not that clearly defined in Iceland: Her father, she said, was "a housewife" for a few years when she was a teenager. Her mother, a nurse, was the breadwinner.

Indeed, the World Economic Forum has ranked Iceland first for gender equality nine years in a row, in an index that examines educational opportunities, life expectancy, pay equity and other factors. Eight out of 10 Icelandic women work, the highest female employment rate in the world.

The pay gap between men and women is due to close here in 2022. The World Economic Forum says that globally, it will take 217 years.

It was starting to snow. The landscape outside was barren, almost moonlike. "You need to be pretty tough to survive in this climate, man and woman," Mr. Prats Monné observed.

He had noticed the sturdy shoes women wore on the plane flight over.

"Iceland is also egalitarian in appearance," he said.

When we arrived at the reception, at a newly built language center dedicated to Vigdis, two dozen women were spilling out of a shuttle bus and into the revolving doors. In his suit and tie amid a sea of colorful dresses and blazers and head scarves, Mr. Prats Monné turned some heads.

The ground floor was packed with women and a sprinkling of men, most of them security guards and journalists. Mr. Prats Monné, a regular at conferences, said the room not only looked different, but sounded different, too: "It's so quiet," he said.

Next to us, two women — a center-left lawmaker from Europe and a conservative one from the Middle East — met for the first time. They hugged and kissed. Mr. Prats Monné mostly shook hands.

"It is a cohesive group that has its own signs and body language," he said, his inner anthropologist emerging. "They acknowledge each other as being from the same tribe. I'm not from their tribe — although I do feel very welcome."

At the buffet, we bumped into Silvana Koch-Mehrin, the founder of Women Political Leaders, the network hosting the summit. Nibbling on a strawberry, Mr. Prats Monné observed: "There really aren't many people who look like me."

"Welcome to my world," Ms. Koch-Mehrin replied.

She set up the network in 2013, because as a female member of the European Parliament she had been painfully conscious of her minority status. "The permanent fashion trial," she sighed, referring to public scrutiny of what prominent women wear.

Mr. Prats Monné has never faced such issues himself. But he empathizes. "There is no such thing as a glass ceiling," he said at one point, "just a big fat layer of men." Of his 35 peers as directorate heads in the European Commission, he noted, only one in five are women.

When he was a student in Madrid 40 years ago, Mr. Prats Monné read the "The Subjection of Women" by John Stuart Mill and was deeply affected by it.

I asked if he is a feminist.

"Of course," he said. "The opposite of feminism is ignorance."

Mr. Prats Monné wanted to know more about the building, a striking modernistic structure, and someone pointed him toward a gentleman in a gray suit.

"The building manager or something," Mr. Prats Monné explained after they spoke.

When I told him later that the man turned out to be the speaker of the Icelandic Parliament, Mr. Prats Monné laughed. "In this setting, when you see a man, you assume he's the janitor."

The next morning, we took seats near a delegation of Jordanian lawmakers and a Greek diplomat. At the next table were the presidents of Lithuania, Malta, Estonia and Croatia. Two tables over were the former prime ministers of Canada and New Zealand. All women.

On the sidelines were half a dozen young men in suits: aides to the delegates, I was told. One held his boss's white coat.

On the agenda: panels on peacekeeping, rape as a weapon of war, (the lack of) women in technology, maternal mortality, sexual harassment.

Yet the first three speakers turned out to be men: Iceland's president, foreign minister and prime minister (who, later in the week, would be replaced by a woman).

Each spoke about how gender equality is their fight, too. They mentioned a 1975 strike, when Iceland's women walked out of factories and kitchens for a day, demanding equal pay, and the subsequent founding of a feminist party. Since then, Iceland, an island of 330,000, has established shared parental leave, banned strip clubs, instituted gender quotas in boardrooms and passed same-sex marriage with a unanimous vote.

Today's global #MeToo movement is claimed by men as much as by women here.

"We men no longer give our tacit approval to sexual harassment," the foreign minister said. The president concurred: "We have had enough."

Iceland is living its own #MeToo moment, after the country's youngest female lawmaker, Aslaug Sigurbjörnsdottir, 27, went on television last week to share her experience: of rumors that she had slept her way up, of a rival candidate putting his hand on her thigh every time he addressed her in front of a room full of students.

An hour after the program aired, Ragnar Önundarson, a banker, had reposted one of her Facebook pictures. "I want you to think about the kind of image you project," he had written.

A day later you could buy T-shirts featuring a troll with the caption "Don't be like Ragnar," and by now 500 people have signed a petition supporting Ms. Sigurbjörnsdottir.

Watching the gathering from Mr. Prats Monné's perspective only underscored its significance, amplifying the subtle signals, sounds, interactions and exchanges that characterized a room filled with powerful women.

When his turn came to speak, it was on a panel with four women. As a health expert, he said he is used to speaking to female audiences, "but usually I'm on a panel of men talking to a female audience."

"Institutionalized mansplaining," he calls it.

Afterward, I asked one of the other panelists if the organizers had invited him onto the panel because they were mindful of diversity.

"No," she assured me, "he is definitely not the token man."

Donald Trump's Gift to Women

BY GAIL COLLINS | DEC. 13, 2017

ON THE DAY before the Alabama election, I found myself explaining that I needed to get to work despite the bombing at my subway station because there were women coming in to talk about having been sexually assaulted by the president.

Really, we live in interesting times.

The bombing — in which no one was seriously hurt but the bomber — has already faded from the memory of New York's hardened mass transit riders. But the rest of the story is reverberating. We're in the middle of a women's uprising that really does feel like a new wave, maybe the one that could actually get the country within shouting distance of power equality.

Think about it. This week Roy Moore got skunked in Alabama, thanks in great part to female voters who went for the Democratic candidate instead. Then the U.S. Senate got ready for another woman member — Minnesota Lt. Gov. Tina Smith is going to replace Al Franken, who is resigning in the sexual harassment scandal.

We have a revolt against sexual harassment that's running through the political, entertainment, restaurant and communications worlds. And we're finally trying to focus on the Donald Trump sleaziness sagas that the nation didn't deal with in 2016. Trump is really behind everything — his election jarred and frightened women so much that there was nothing to do but rebel and try to change the world.

"I think it's very much because of President Trump," said Senator Kirsten Gillibrand of New York. "For me the Women's March was still the most extraordinary political moment of my lifetime." Gillibrand is a leader of the antiharassment campaign in Congress. This week, as some of the women who had stories about Trump's own hands-on history were talking to the media, she called on the president to resign.

Trump responded — as only he can — with a Twitter attack, calling Gillibrand a political "lightweight" who used to come to him "begging" for campaign contributions, "and would do anything for them."

"I think it was intended to be a sexist smear, and it was intended to silence me and every woman who challenges him," Gillibrand said in a phone interview.

The White House retorted that only a person whose mind was "in the gutter" would think the president was talking about anything but the way political fund-raising means "special interests control our government."

What do you think, people? Perhaps we could just do a calculation on how much time Trump has spent in his public life discussing girl-grabbing versus campaign finance reform.

Also, no one in Washington seems to have missed the fact that when the president tweeted, Gillibrand was at a congressional Bible study meeting.

It's for sure that when Donald Trump beat Hillary Clinton it triggered a visceral response in masses of American women, and that trauma may be turning into a political uprising more powerful than the Tea Party. Women voters delivered Alabama for Democrat Doug Jones — 57 percent came down on his side. The critical mass actually came from the African-American community, where women vote more faithfully than men, and virtually all of them went for Jones. (Hard to know what triggered their outpouring — Roy Moore's creepy sexual history or his enthusiasm for the good old days of strong families and slavery.)

"I see black women as the heart of the Democratic Party," said Gillibrand.

Other women aren't exactly standing still. A new Monmouth University poll has Trump's job approval rating down to another new historic low, 32 percent. The decline, Monmouth said, came mostly from Republican and independent women. All in all, women gave the president thumbs-up only 24 percent of the time. He's their political equivalent of overcooked broccoli.

We truly could be seeing a new wave of feminist reform. The United States has had moments when it looked as if women were finally taking their rightful place in the public world. But things had a way of stalling. After suffrage wars, politicians were worried about pleasing their new female constituents. But they then concluded that women were going to pretty much vote like their male relatives, and lost interest. The "Year of the Woman" in 1992 added four more U.S. senators to the pair of women who were already there. But now, in the 21st century, the Senate still has only 21.

There could be a lot more if this revolution continues. And while we have no earthly idea who the Democratic presidential candidate will be in 2020, it's likely that a bunch of women are going to be in the mix — Gillibrand probably among them.

Think about it. The only Democratic woman who's ever been a top-of-the-pack presidential contender was Hillary Clinton, a former first lady. And I can remember being around when it was a big deal that Margaret Chase Smith got her name put into nomination at the Republican convention after a campaign dominated by dissection of her muffin recipe.

It's not necessarily bad when the times get interesting.

One Year After Women's March, More Activism but Less Unity

BY FARAH STOCKMAN | JAN. 15, 2018

Women's March Inc., which organized the event in Washington, has encouraged more protests. But a new group is focused on winning elections, especially in red states.

AMBER SELMAN-LYNN wanted to help plan a women's march in Mobile, Ala., this month to mark the first anniversary of last year's huge protests across the country. The day had been significant for her.

With no experience in political activism, she had helped organize a bus full of women to go from Mobile to Washington. After they came back from the euphoric trip, they formed a group called Mobile Marchers that met monthly. They spoke up for the Affordable Care Act at town-hall-style meetings, and knocked on doors for the Alabama Senate candidate Doug Jones, the Democrat who beat Roy S. Moore in a stunning victory last month.

But when Ms. Selman-Lynn tried to register her anniversary event on the website for Women's March Inc., the high-profile group formed by the organizers of last year's event in Washington, she received an unusual letter. It said that while the group was "supportive of any efforts to build our collective power as women," it asked that she "not advertise your event as a 'Women's March' action."

"It's kind of silly," Ms. Selman-Lynn said. "We are clearly the women's march in Mobile."

The Women's March a year ago aimed to start a movement of women from all walks of life who would continue their activism long after they had gone home.

In many ways, that goal has been realized. In the wake of the march on Washington — and simultaneous marches in more than 600 towns and cities across the country — thousands of women threw themselves into activism for the first time in their lives, especially in red states where the events provided a rare chance to build a network of like-minded people.

In Texas, emails collected by the organizers of the Women's March in Austin are being repurposed to promote candidates who support abortion rights. In Arkansas, Gwen Combs, the elementary school-teacher who organized the Little Rock march, is now running for Congress. Thousands of women in October attended a convention in Detroit training them on everything from lobbying elected officials to confronting white supremacy.

But as the movement evolves, differing priorities and tactics have emerged among the women, nearly all of them unpaid and spread across the country. Now, on the eve of the anniversary, a rift is emerging between two groups: Women's March Inc., which organized the march on Washington and spent much of the year creating more social justice protests, and another organization of activists who planned sister marches last year and believe that winning elections, particularly in red states, should be the primary goal. The split has raised questions about who can claim the mantle of the Women's March — and the funding and press attention that goes with it.

The newer group, named March On, formed after some female activists in red states felt the protests being encouraged by Women's March Inc., which is based in New York, were not resonating in their communities.

"We can march and take to the streets and yell about all the stuff we want to change, but unless we're getting people elected to office who are going to make those changes, we're not really doing anything," said Lindsey Kanaly, who organized the women's march in Oklahoma City and is now a March On board member.

The group is now focused on helping liberal women in Republican-led districts organize ahead of the pivotal midterm elections this year.

Mindful of the optics of dividing the movement, March On founders describe the organization as a complement, not a competitor, to Women's March Inc. Both groups have refrained from criticizing the other in

TODD HEISLER/THE NEW YORK TIMES

The organizers of the march in Washington chose leaders from communities that have historically been ignored by mainstream feminist groups. From left, the national co-chairwomen are Tamika Mallory, Linda Sarsour, Bob Bland and Carmen Perez.

public. But behind the scenes, there has been some frustration.

Winnie Wong, a Women's March Inc. volunteer and adviser, wrote recently in a public Facebook post that March On "seems like an ill-conceived attempt at organized co-option."

"Somebody got to tell the truth!" replied Tamika Mallory, a co-president of Women's March Inc.

Bob Bland, also a co-president, said the new group was "welcome in the resistance." But she noted that its creation had led to "a lot of confusion" among activists on the ground who did not realize that it was a separate entity.

"That's why it is so important for new groups coming into this movement, like March On, to make sure they have distinct branding and messaging that is specific to them and their group that doesn't appear as if it is directly Women's March related," Ms. Bland said.

Ms. Selman-Lynn in Mobile had been unaware of the difference between the two groups and organized her event using online tools from March On. To satisfy Women's March Inc., she reprinted her banner to remove March On's slogan, "March On the Polls."

It was a minor inconvenience, she said. But she hopes the two groups will work together in the future.

"The Women's March is really iconic and of course we want to be a part of that," she said. "But March On has a great tool kit. Most of us have never done this before. We need all the guidance we can get."

The dispute over branding gives a glimpse of how much has changed since ad hoc committees of volunteers put together the marches in the weeks after President Trump's election.

The marches grew out of a Facebook post by a woman in Hawaii who floated the idea, attracting widespread interest. A core group of organizers in New York City planned the march on Washington, while hundreds of other women organized similar marches in their own communities.

The organizers of the march in Washington made a point of picking leaders from communities who have historically been ignored by mainstream feminist groups. Of the four national co-chairwomen of the Washington march, three were minorities. But the group's leadership had very little geographic diversity. Nearly all of the board members of Women's March Inc. are from New York City.

After the march, Women's March Inc. used its powerful platform to advance social justice causes, urging marchers to hold conversations about racial injustice, protest the deportation of undocumented immigrants, attend vigils for Syria and participate in a national strike called A Day Without Women. Women's March Inc. activists said they saw social justice protests as crucial to forming effective and diverse coalitions.

Yet many of their protests failed to catch on in red states.

"What they are doing is great, but it's difficult to tap into here," said Kelly Smith, a librarian from Berea, Ky., who organized buses from Kentucky to Washington for the march last year. A general strike could not work in Kentucky, a state where many women depend on hourly wages and do not have union protections, she said.

Women "would have come back to work the next day and had no job," she said. "I can't be on board with that."

Kentuckians have other urgent priorities, like saving the pensions of public-school teachers that were cut by a conservative governor, she said.

In Texas, Melissa Fiero, who helped organize a march of 100,000 people in Austin, said her group had not participated in any of the protests urged by Women's March Inc. Instead, it has focused on promoting Democrats for local office.

"The needs are different from Texas to New York," said Ms. Fiero, who lives in the rural community of Oatmeal. "A woman's right to choose is constantly under assault in Texas."

Both Ms. Kelly and Ms. Fiero have chosen to affiliate with March On.

The goal of March On is to take a "bottom-up" approach that can draw women in rural places, said Jaquie Algee, who helped plan the Women's March in Chicago and now serves as the board chairwoman of March On.

"We wanted to make sure that women in red states who need the most support are in positions of leadership," said Ms. Algee, who is also an organizer in Kansas, Indiana and Missouri for the Service Employees International Union. Ms. Algee, who is black, said that March On also "strives continually" for racial diversity in its leadership. Four out of 13 board members are minorities.

Ms. Bland disputes claims that Women's March Inc. has had difficulty in conservative areas. "Red states are where there's actually the most activity," she said. "We're here to facilitate the vision of the actual state organizers and the grass-roots groups that are doing the work."

March On's founders say the group grew out of weekly conference calls held by the organizers of sister marches as they swapped tips on applying for permits, finding sponsors and obtaining event insurance. After the marches, they met for the first time at a retreat and decided to form a new organization that would focus on giving organizers tools to help win elections.

ALYSSA SCHUKAR FOR THE NEW YORK TIMES

Jaquie Algee, a March On board member, at a planning meeting for the 2018 "March on the Polls" event in Chicago.

In October, March On began an initiative called March on the Polls, which urges local activists to use the anniversary to help register and educate voters in advance of the midterm elections.

Two months later, in December, Women's March Inc. announced its own campaign called "Power to the Polls," with an opening rally in Las Vegas on Jan. 21.

Women's March Inc. has struggled to bring the decentralized women's march movement under its umbrella.

Before the march, the Women's March logo, created by Nicole LaRue, a designer who worked pro bono, was shared freely with groups all over the world. Since then, Women's March Inc. has tried to exert greater control over who can use it.

Canadian activists who held marches in solidarity with the Women's March on Washington were outraged when American activists with Women's March Inc. in New York registered the name Women's

March Canada and appointed a board without consulting them.

"We believe our network has shown itself to be excellent custodians of the Women's March spirit and ethos, and respectfully request the time and space to prepare a plan to move ahead in unity and solidarity," they wrote in an open letter to national co-chairwomen of the Women's March on Washington.

After they did not get a response, they renamed themselves March On Canada and created the Twitter hashtag #DontTradeMarkTheMovement. They are now affiliated with, but not controlled by, March On.

Jo Reger, professor of sociology at Oakland University in Michigan, says the feminist movement, like other important social movements, has always had people coming together and then breaking apart.

"We think it looks so chaotic and full of factions and what it really looks like is every other social movement," Dr. Reger said. "Often those factions end up coming back together later on."

So far, the split between Women's March and March On has not dampened the enthusiasm for marking the anniversary. Many activists in the field said they were unaware of the division. Those who are say they seek resources from both organizations: Women's March Inc. provides a unifying vision and a national spotlight, while March On gives on-the-ground support, such as legal advice on applying for nonprofit status.

Many women say the marches last year unleashed a new era of activism and a level of energy that shows no sign of flagging. Ms. Selman-Lynn said she simply wanted all the help she could get to win more elections for Democrats in Alabama.

"We have a lot of work to do, convincing people that there's a grass-roots group with a lot of energy who is willing to work," said Ms. Selman-Lynn. "We've got a lot of ground to gain here."

Money Is Power. And Women Need More of Both.

BY SUSAN CHIRA | MARCH 10, 2018

WOMEN ARE RUNNING for political office in record numbers this year. They are challenging the sexual status quo from Hollywood to corporate offices, pursuing power as seldom before.

But there is one barrier yet to be toppled: Money.

Of 2,043 billionaires on the latest annual Forbes tally, 227 are women; most of that small group inherited their wealth.

A record number of women were donors and political bundlers for Hillary Clinton's campaign, but men still gave the most money and were the largest individual donors. Parents spent more time talking about money with boys than with girls last year, according to a survey conducted by T. Rowe Price.

For all the heady anticipation about women winning midterm elections and female voters demanding change, it's the influence that comes with money that endures. "Political power is ephemeral," said Alicia Glen, New York's deputy mayor for housing and economic development, who was a managing director at Goldman Sachs. "People can just wait you out. But if you're the richest person on the planet, there's no waiting you out."

Yet many women, those who grew up wealthy and those who did not, have long been steered away from the unapologetic drive for wealth.

It's bound up with the way girls are often schooled to place the needs of others above their own, to repress or deny outward signs of ambition. Even as women have pushed into once-male bastions in business, many still feel the sting of professional and personal backlash if they are perceived as too aggressive.

"Girls as they are growing up are not socialized to feel that it's O.K. for them to have ambition about creating wealth, not the way it is for little boys," said Mariko Chang, the author of "Shortchanged," a study

CHLOE SCHEFFE

of the wealth gap between men and women. "They're encouraged to take on roles that let them take care of other people."

Joline Godfrey, author of the book "Raising Financially Fit Kids" and a California-based education consultant, coaches families on how to avoid sending a dismissive message to girls about money. For example, if a girl proposes a lemonade stand, take her seriously and help her talk about a business plan, rather than pronouncing her cute. Parents are often more likely to reward boys for accomplishments or risk-taking while urging girls to be careful.

Families want help navigating this terrain, yet old attitudes die hard. Ms. Godfrey recalls a talk she gave a few years ago to a group of very wealthy families, posing questions about what they most wanted for their sons and then their daughters, including financial success, good careers and personal happiness. For their sons, the families' answers ranged widely among these attributes. But virtually every family chose personal happiness for their daughters above anything else.

Indeed, the most bracing scene in "Equity," a film about women on Wall Street that opened during the 2016 presidential campaign, is when the dealmaker Naomi Bishop (played by Anna Gunn) states baldly, "I like money."

It was a jaw-dropping moment because such portrayals are so rare — and that void is one that Sarah Megan Thomas, one of the film's writers, stars and producers, set out to fill, with financial backing from a group of Wall Street women. "We don't show strong women liking money on screen," she said.

Irene Chang Britt spent 30 years at Fortune 500 companies, six of them in the executive suite. She trained as an anthropologist, but said her mother also pushed her to get an M.B.A. She ascended the corporate ladder by proving she could increase profits in the divisions she led, so money was a direct measure of her achievements. "Money motivated me, for sure," she said. "But for me it's more about accomplishment and power than money."

At the same time, Ms. Britt says she thinks women are often discouraged from openly promoting themselves and the money they make or generate in the way men are allowed to do.

"Money is a form of praise, and you're deflecting that praise," she said, summarizing the message she thinks women often receive. "It's not ladylike, and you won't attract a guy."

Even when women do make substantial money, they have often chosen to exercise the influence it brings differently from men.

From her perches both in investment banking and city government, Ms. Glen has watched men relish the rewards money brings. She pointed out that men outnumber women on many of the most powerful boards of New York, including its major hospitals, the Metropolitan Museum of Art and the Real Estate Board of New York. "I'm on the board of Mount Sinai, so I can get your cousin in to see the best doctor," she said, describing the currency of board membership for some wealthy men.

Many women I interviewed said they viewed money as a means to help others rather than to increase their own profile. Those attitudes, admirable as they may be, have helped fuel a power gap that separates men and women.

Of course, many recoil at the idea that women should pursue money and clout just the way men do. That flies in the face of increasing political anger about inequality. There's a longstanding rift in the women's movement and beyond: Does the path to power require acting more like men, or can women wield influence in ways that are different but just as effective?

"There are men for whom there is no amount of money that is enough," Ms. Godfrey said. "The quest of more, bigger, better has taken this planet to a place of unsustainability. It seems to me that women are making different choices. And those choices may be healthier for all of us."

Diana L. Taylor has spent years on Wall Street, in state government, and on corporate and philanthropic boards. That experience, as well as being the partner of a former New York City mayor, Michael R. Bloomberg, has given her a close-up view of both political power and great wealth.

When she graduated from Dartmouth in 1977, she said, her father refused to pay for business school. "He said, 'Why bother?' " she recalled. " 'You'll just get married and have kids.' " So she paid her own way through business school, won over her father and landed in investment banking. She left one firm to start another one in the late 1980s when she learned she was being paid less than men at her level.

Women have long been active philanthropists, but Ms. Taylor observed that women tend to give to smaller organizations that might not offer the flashiest rewards for donors.

Research suggests that men continue to set priorities and reap more direct power from philanthropy than women. Ms. Chang found that women were more likely to use their wealth to help other people, and men to advance their influence, such as naming a building or donating to a college. "Women have not been socialized to brag and have their names on things," said Debra Mesch, director of the Women's Philanthropy Institute at Indiana University.

However they exercise it, more women appear to be awakening to the power wealth can endow.

Male political donors like Tom Steyer on the left and the Koch brothers on the right have been able to force issues they champion onto their parties' agendas. There are far fewer women with the kind of wealth that buys impact on that scale — although more are mobilizing. Among those women is Rebekah Mercer, who has deployed her family's fortune to press the causes she wants Republicans to embrace.

In 2017, nearly four times the number of women donated to political campaigns than in the two years of the previous midterm cycle, according to preliminary results analyzed by the Center for Responsive Politics. More women have given money to congressional campaigns in this cycle than men, primarily to Democratic candidates, according to a Crowdpac analysis.

Even if they are ambivalent about the pursuit of money, women are increasingly fed up with persistent pay gaps and are demanding that they be paid as much as men for the same work. Carrie Gracie shamed the BBC by quitting when she saw the gap between her salary as China editor and those of men she considered peers. Out of the limelight, many women are sharing details of their salaries, breaching taboos against honest talk about money.

Sarah Elliott is a 33-year-old advertising sales executive in an entertainment and gaming company who looks to Ms. Britt, the former Fortune 500 executive, as a mentor. She said when she entered advertising as a research analyst, she was following her interests rather than focusing on her salary. About five years in, she realized that she was providing research to help close deals but was earning far less than her colleagues in sales. "Why am I not getting the financial benefits of all this work?" she recalled thinking. "In sales, the harder you work the more money you make."

Now she belongs to a network of women her age who exchange salary information. She is investing in Plum Alley, one of several networks of women-owned businesses that are attracting female investors. And this is the first year she's considered political donations, inspired by the number of women running for office.

Ms. Glen, the deputy mayor, said the young women in business she mentors are growing impatient with the slow, halting climb to the top of corporate America and are choosing entrepreneurship instead. "Young women aren't looking toward Wall Street but toward billion-dollar I.P.O.s," she said.

But not, at least for now, her own daughter. Set against women's growing boldness about money is a resentment over inequality and corporate influence. Ms. Glen's daughter, a college senior, told her mother that she had no intention of working at a for-profit company. "I get why she feels that way," Ms. Glen said. "But I want to make sure she's not disempowering herself. I want her to be a badass."

In 2016, many women who believed they were on the cusp of electing the first female president took their daughters with them to the polls. Outrage on the left at Donald J. Trump's election drove many women toward political activism and to run for office themselves. Perhaps their daughters may grow up not just to aspire to be candidates — but to bankroll them.

SUSAN CHIRA (@SUSANCHIRA) IS A SENIOR CORRESPONDENT AND EDITOR ON GENDER ISSUES FOR THE NEW YORK TIMES.

CHAPTER 5

Society, Sex and Relationships

As women's roles have changed over time, so have the social and sexual norms associated with them. What it meant to be a mid-19th-century wife was entirely different from what's expected of a spouse today. Margaret Sanger's dedication to making birth control widely available empowered women to regulate whether and how many children they had. The roaring 1920s ushered in the era of the flapper — independent women who bucked convention by valuing a good time above all else. Women began to marry after finishing college, establishing a career, or not at all. Sexual harassment and date rape gained greater notice. And women continue to contemplate what role they play in today's world.

It Is Not A Woman's Right.

BY THE NEW YORK TIMES | DEC. 16, 1852.

WE BELIEVE IN women's rights, and it is a part of our creed that they should have all that is their own. We would shame the stout, strong men from behind counters, where tape and needles and lace are sold; out of schoolrooms where young ideas could so much better be taught to shoot by females than by males; out of every office and position that belongs by the common consent to the ladies; out of the medical offices even, if they are silly and self-denying enough, willingly to enter them; but, — ah! it sorely grieves our gallantry that we must plead the rights of woman with a *but* — but then we have our little rights too, which we would far rather surrender at discretion than under compulsion.

Now, when we have gone a full hour before the opening of a lecture that we might be sure of a good seat, having paid for our ticket full price, and being no "dead head" at all, and the lecturer has gone through with his introduction and is just warming up with his glowing sentences — to have the prettiest-looking Miss in town enter slowly and march directly to our seat, *because it is the best*, and hint as distinctly as possible that we must come out of it and spend the remainder of the evening in standing first on one foot and then on the other, mingling unpleasant reflections on our own uneasiness, with the sallies of wit from the platform, savage meditations on the impudence of the beauty that ousted us, with the speaker's genial thoughts, to which it is impossible to listen any longer comfortably — we say that when we are thus maltreated, we feel very much tempted to ask women to defend their position, and to pin them down to their rights and nothing else. We hold that all men were born free and equal to women in the right to enjoy a good seat at concert, sermon, or lecture, when it has been honorably secured at first.

As to the physiology of the matter, ladies are far more commonly than men given to sedentary habits, and a little standing does them good; while the stronger sex, having spent their days in sterner occupations, need the rest of a comfortable seat.

And now, if that lady reads the *Times*, who came into the Harlem cars, the other night, and compelled — yes, compelled — us to vacate our seat, that she might be accommodated, — for it is nothing short of compulsion, when a female, whether clothed in tatters or in velvet and furs, takes up her position close by us and looks as if the very seat we occupy were hers by every title — we say if she will condescend to thank us the next time we put ourselves to so sore an inconvenience for her sex's sake, we will repeat the favor with the greatest good will. Mind, we do not say that hereafter we *will* have our seat whether a lady is standing or not. It is not probable we could hold out if we should resolve ever so strongly upon that. But if we have been walking for three or four hours it marvellously mitigates the tedium of standing, to receive the smile of the lady we accommodate with our seat. A little common politeness on the part of the accommodated lends a staff to one who is weary — a simple "thank you," is nearly as good as a cushioned armchair. The point is this: if we pay for a seat in a railroad car, we are entitled to it quite as much as if we wore skirts and a mantilla. The very best privilege of the possession is the right it affords us to give it away to the first modest-looking lady who cannot find as good a one. And we cannot consent to have it taken from us as if we were intruders, and only occupying it on sufferance even by the belle of the village or the daughter of the rich Squire.

The Old Wife and the New

BY THE NEW YORK TIMES | SEPT. 19, 1897

ONE WAS A kitchen drudge, and the other is a homemaker and her husband's friend.

One is Mrs. John Smith, the other is Mrs. Mary Smith. The former is rapidly becoming an extinct genus. In a few decades, perhaps, as some social scientists tell us, the places that have known her so long will know her no more forever, and in her stead we have Mrs. Mary Smith, a creature so different from Mrs. John Smith that it is hard to believe that both were women who belonged to the same race and lived in the same century. So nearly gone is that former Mrs. Smith that one unconsciously speaks of her in the past tense.

Mrs. John Smith was usually a sad-eyed, subdued woman whose life meant a degree of toil and self-abnegation that made her a pale, colorless shadow of what she might have been. She worked early and late, grew old before her time, and found in her children and grandchildren a sort of vicarious happiness that scarcely took the place of the real happiness she expected when she stood up before the minister and promised to be John Smith's wife.

Mrs. Mary Smith, on the other hand, is a cheerful, somewhat aggressive sort of personality, who combines a proper regard for others with an equally proper regard for herself. Strangers tell her she looks as young as her married daughter, and John Smith often declares she grows prettier every year of her life. She loves her children, but she has, too, an existence quite apart from them, and enjoys all the luxury of living that belongs nowadays to a thoroughly individualized woman.

Mrs. John Smith's recreation consisted in going to church on Sundays, to prayer meeting on Wednesday nights, and to the Sewing Society Friday afternoons. Once or twice a year, at Christmas or Thanksgiving, she had all of John's folks and her own to dinner, and once or twice a year the minister and his wife would come to tea. Mrs.

Mary Smith is not indifferent to the claims of the Church, but between the Sundays of life she stows away a wholesome amount of concerts and calls and plays and operas that keep her in touch with music, art, and society, and when she entertains, it is a pleasure and not a stern, back-breaking duty, as in the olden time.

Mrs. John Smith was a very economical woman. She darned and patched and planned and contrived and made things over and wore old dresses and bonnets in a pathetic defiance of fashion. Now and then in some dire extremity of personal need she would summon up courage to ask John for "a little money," and if John happened to be a cross, ill-tempered brute, she bore his growls at her extravagance with the divine patience that was the badge of womanhood in that day. Mrs. Mary Smith is not unlearned in domestic economy — to say nothing of social and political economy. She understands the fine art of putting a new seat in little Johnny's trousers and closing with fine needlework the holes in big John's socks. But she believes there is such a thing as economy of eyesight, nerve power, and precious time, and knows that she is of far more importance to John and the children than a lot of old clothes. She gives the old garments to some one to whom they are a godsend, and naps and walks to the great improvement of her nerves and complexion. She believes that one of woman's chief duties is to dress as stylishly as she possibly can, especially after marriage, and she has her separate purse, as a matter of course, just as she has a separate tooth brush and hair brush and comb. John would as soon think of questioning her right to the latter as to the former.

WHERE MRS. JOHN'S MISTAKE WAS MADE.

Mrs. John Smith meekly promised to obey her husband. She kept the promise until death released her from it, and it was the keeping of the promise that caused the death.

Mrs. Mary Smith looks around until she finds a minister who is man enough to leave out the word "obey" at the marriage ceremony, and John realizes at the start that he is in possession of a wife, but not a slave.

Mrs. John Smith knew the days of the week as wash day, ironing day, scrubbing day, churning day, mending day, and baking day, and each one of these laid a separate and distinct ache for her back and her head. She belonged to the Dorcas Society, the Mite Society, and the Missionary Society, and went to them whenever she had time. Mrs. Mary Smith is President of the Browning Club, Vice President of the Nineteenth Century Club, Secretary of a Woman's Municipal league and Director of a Kindergarten or two. She reckons the days of the week according to the meetings of these organizations, and she thinks it a deadly sin for a mother to do work that would cause a backache or a headache.

Mrs. John Smith was a celebrated cook. She could make sixteen kinds of cake, and eleven kinds of pie, and the neighbors all borrowed her receipts for pickles and preserves. Mrs. Mary Smith has studied cooking as a fine art, and she practices that art at intervals, as she paints and embroiders. But she knows that no woman can be a kitchen drudge and at the same time a home-maker, a wife, and a mother.

Mrs. John Smith, dressed in brown, gray and black, and considered herself an elderly woman after her second child was born. Mrs. Mary Smith wears the colors that her eighteen-year-old daughter wears, and has serious dreams of perpetual youth.

Mrs. John Smith's artistic work took the form of wax flowers, worsted embroidery, and much crocheting. Mrs. Mary Smith paints china, models in clay, and does rare Kensington work.

Mrs. John Smith sent her boys to college and kept her girls at home, trusting devoutly that Providence would provide each one with a husband. Mrs. Mary Smith sends her girls to college along with their brothers, and sometimes, with John's consent, she goes with them and takes a special course in something that particularly interests her.

Mrs. John Smith's husband always called her "mother," and when he wanted to talk to anybody he went away from home. Mrs. Mary's husband calls her "wife" and an hour of her society is the richest treat in the world for him.

Mrs. John believed that women should have privileges — if they could get them; Mrs. Mary believes that women should have rights, and she takes hers with self-possession and aplomb.

A BELATED CANONIZATION.

When Mrs. John dies the minister tells of her patience and long-suffering in the midst of her manifold trials and tribulations, celebrates the great number of her children and grandchildren, and calls her "a mother in Israel." When Mrs. Mary dies a half dozen clubs pass resolutions, and her obituary notices are in as many newspapers.

But why multiply these antitheses? Everybody is familiar with the two types, and everybody knows they are the setting and the rising stars in the social firmament. Each has her admirers and advocates. There be some who look on Mrs. Mary as a dangerous and revolutionary individual, and lament that all the Mrs. Smiths cannot be Mrs. Johns. Others are of a divided mind. They realize the virtues of Mrs. John, and when they think of the thorny way she trod, want to do what they can toward canonizing her. The style of her name is a great obstacle in the way of this, however. She was always "Mrs. John," and nothing more, and if one puts the appellation of "Saint" before the given name — Mrs. Saint John Smith — it will appear to be canonizing John, whereas it is his wife that should be canonized, and as for John, if anything is done for him, it would be to anathematize him most likely. This is one of the minor disadvantages that befall a woman who discards her own name; she can never be properly canonized.

The advocates of Mrs. Mary would probably claim saintly honors for her, too, and when one surveys her good deeds and her fair, busy life in public and in private, he is likely to concede the claim. But so much of "honor, profit, and emolument" belongs to Mrs. Mary already that canonizing would really be a superfluity.

Mrs. John had her day. Mrs. Mary is having hers, and the world can no more prevent the passing of the former type and the evolution of the latter than it can stay the passing of the aboriginal Indian and prevent the march of the world's progress.

Mrs. Sanger Defies Courts Before 3,000

BY THE NEW YORK TIMES | JAN. 30, 1917

THREE THOUSAND PERSONS in mass meeting at Carnegie Hall last night started a concerted movement for the repeal of the law forbidding the dissemination of birth control knowledge.

Mrs. Margaret Sanger, in whose trial for conducting a birth control clinic decision was reserved in Brooklyn yesterday, made a speech in which she threw all caution aside and removed all doubt as to her purpose when she declared, while the crowd cheered her wildly, that she had devoted her life to the cause of voluntary motherhood, and would continue to fight for birth control, courts or no courts, workhouse or no workhouse. Mrs. Sanger, is a sister of Mrs. Ethel Byrne, who is on a hunger strike in the Blackwell's Island workhouse, serving a thirty days' sentence.

Most of the crowd were women — women of all classes, old, young, poor, and rich. The two upper galleries were filled, because the admission charge there was only 25 cents. The admission on the lower floor, which was two-thirds filled, was 75 cents. The boxes, which were allotted by subscription, were filled with richly dressed persons, many of them socially prominent. The money from the admissions, with deductions for the hall, went for a fund to pay lawyers to fight the anti-birth control measure in the courts and at Albany. The leaders of the "cause" said that if it had not rained and kept away poor people the hall would have been filled.

There was no age limit to the admission. Many girls were in the audience who might have keen high school students — few of them had escorts. The spirit of the crowd was bubbling. Every mention of the name of Mrs. Sanger and of Mrs. Byrne brought prolonged cheers.

POLICE DO NOT INTERFERE.

The promoters of the meeting had expected trouble with the police over the distribution of the first number of The Birth Control Review, published by the New York State Birth Control League. But no one interfered while the ushers sold the magazine at 15 cents a copy.

Dr. Mary Hunt, a well-known physician, made an attack on "Fifth Avenue doctors," who, she said, practiced birth control in their own families and in the families of their rich patients, but stood in the way of poor women obtaining that knowledge.

Miss Helen Todd, who presided, introduced Mrs. Sanger as a woman who, "with Mrs. Byrne was making a bridge over which womankind could pass to freedom."

It was noted that Mrs. Sanger departed from the prepared copy of her speech in that she was not so severe on the judiciary as she had intended to be. She had evidently prepared her speech in the conviction that she was to be found guilty yesterday afternoon.

"I come to you tonight," she said, "from a crowded courtroom, from a vortex of persecution. I come not from the stake of Salem, where women were burned for blasphemy, but from the shadow of Blackwell's Island, where women are tortured for 'obscenity.'

EMANCIPATION FOR WORKERS.

"Birth control is the one means by which the working man shall find emancipation. I was one of eleven children. My mother died when I was 17 because she had had too many children and had worked herself to death. I became a nurse to help support my family, and I soon discovered that 75 per cent of the diseases of men and women are due to sex ignorance. I determined that when I was able I would do what I could to solve that problem. I found that the average person was as ignorant of sex matters as our most primitive ancestors. There has been progress in every department of our lives except in the most important — creation. So I came to the conclusion that the greatest good I could do was to help poor women to have fewer children to be brought up in want and poverty. I threw my nurse's bag away and swore I would take it up no more. I went to Europe and studied the birth control clinics there and came back to American to do what I could.

"Colonel Roosevelt goes all about the country telling people to have large families and he is neither arrested nor molested. But can he tell me why I got sixty-three letters in one week from poor mothers in Oyster Bay asking me for birth control information? No woman can call herself free until she can choose the time she will become a mother.

"My purpose in life is to arouse sentiment of the repeal of the law, State and Federal. It is we women who have paid for the folly of this law, and it is up to us to repeal it. It is only by birth control that woman can prepare with man, her brother, for the emancipation of the race."

Dr. Mary Hunt said there were three classes of women for whom birth control seemed to her imperative — the tubercular woman, and those with kidney and heart disease and the insane.

"And I, the doctor, am told that I cannot help these women," she added. "What sort of law is that?" I have every regard for the little woman with the great soul down there on Blackwell's Island fighting a fight for all women.

"The great injustice of the situation was shown the other night at the meeting of the County Medical Society when one of the doctors who opposed birth control said on the floor that he practiced it, and at any time was liable to indictment and imprisonment. He told the truth. And what is more, the doctors of New York practice in their own families what they deny less fortunate families. The average child rate of a large number of physicians in New York, all married on an average of sixteen years, was found to be about one child. They practice birth control among the women who can pay for it, and the poor women can go hang. But down on the east side, where my clinic is, we cannot do those things, because the woman policeman would soon find it out and arrest us, and we could do no more of the good we now do."

Miss Todd read a set of resolutions which said in part:

Resolved, That we unqualifiedly condemn the action of the District Attorney and judicial officers of Kings County in denying to Mrs. Sanger her right to trial by jury and to Mrs. Byrne a stay of sentence pending her appeal to a higher court, and also refusing to hear medical and sociological testimony so that these cases might be tried on the merits of the vital human issues involved and not on legal technicalities.

Resolved, That we extend our deepest sympathy to that brave champion of the American womanhood, Ethel Byrne, in her martyrdom for birth control, and protest vigorously against the cruel and arbitrary action of the Commissioner of Correction, Burdette G. Lewis, in denying to her friends and relative access to her bedside.

Resolved, That we declare our firm determination to do our utmost to secure such change in State and Federal laws as shall put birth control knowledge within the reach of all who need it.

Resolved, That we pledge to Margaret Sanger our unwavering moral and financial support in her campaign, to establish the principle of voluntary motherhood in this country.

Relative to the subject matter the resolution, it may be said that Mrs. Sanger has been indicted by a Grand Jury, and will have a trial by jury, in addition to the Special Sessions hearing, and also that at the trial yesterday Presiding Justice Freschi did ask for medical testimony, which was not forthcoming from either side.

More Ado About the Flapper

BY MARGARET O'LEARY | APRIL 16, 1922

CONCERN — and consternation — about the flapper are general. She disports herself flagrantly in the public eye, and there is no keeping her out of grown-up company or conversation. Roughly, the world is divided into those who delight in her, those who fear her and those who try pathetically to take her as a matter of course. Optimists have called her the hope of a the new era, pessimists point to her as ultimate evidence of the decadence of the old.

Curiously, even quaintly, approval of this newest and outwardly outrageous example of social insubordination is apt to come from persons who habitually frown on frivolity, while and old-fashioned prejudice against her is discovered lurking the breasts of people whom Dr. Straton would doubtless count among her natural allies and champions — those dreadful stage people, especially.

There was Laurette Taylor, for example, who complains that she can't get rid of the ghost of "Peg o' My Heart," though she has been, theatrically, since Peg died, a Red Cross nurse, and Italian fortune teller and is now the lamentable lady who takes to drink and jazz in spite of herself in Hartley Manners's play "The National Anthem."

"You were speaking of flappers," she said. "Truly I don't know what a flapper is. You see," Laurette smiled wistfully, "I am at the play every evening. While the world dines I work, and while the world works I dine, so that I rarely see a flapper. To my mind the word bring the image of a little rich girl. She must be young, of course, quite young, 16, 17, 18, a young little thing flapping her wings, adroitly, awkwardly perhaps, aspiringly, and she must be rich or she wouldn't have time to be a flapper; in short, the sort of thing one sees at the Ritz, the Plaza or the Biltmore at tea."

It was timidly suggested that there were lots of flappers who weren't rich — beginning young female artists, superior office girls, professional or pseudo-professional girls, 'prentice writers, precocious lady bums, or what not. They also were seen flapping about. During the day, to be sure, they are engaged more or less seriously upon other concerns, but when the magic hour strikes they emerge like butterflies from cocoons. From the office, the studio, the apartment, the school they flit, as expensively fur-coated as the idle daughters of the rich themselves, and as well — or better — furnished with dancing partners. Flappers these, also, but not without a purpose which may be a serious and important as that of the superior brand of the tribe revealed to Miss Virginia Potter after years of uplift work among girls. Some of them, like as not, are Miss Potter's very own flappers. But the purpose of their flapping is collecting — collecting and still collecting — a male clientele — in short, beaux. Collecting them and trying them out with a view to selection — natural selection — if you will. Eventually, matrimonial selection.

Miss Taylor held up eloquent hands of horror.

"I don't call those flappers," said the ex-Peg; "they are fast young persons. A good girl would be content with one man. She would collect him and begin her real job. Your flapper — if you call her that — can't work or study all day and dance all night and make good at what she works at." The tone might have been Mrs. Grundy's very own.

A murmur to the effect that as a matter of fact many young persons did seem to get away with such a program set the actress off on the theme of her own play — the jazz peril.

"You may remember," she said, "my line in 'The National Anthem.' I say, 'I'm sick of seeing young people dance around as though they couldn't help it. It's not dancing but a series of collisions.' Now, I do really think this jazz is a menace to the country. From the point of view of health, it is poisonous, nerve-racking, shattering, the din and clatter, the tomtom music — no rhythm, no melody — just sex and bedlam! And the young men! My word! As one of them is made to say in the play, 'If you don't drink, I don't see what you do with yourself.'"

Miss Taylor pulled up in mid-career and smiled: "Please don't think I am taking a high moral tone about this thing. I've already said

I don't know anything about flappers and I am not really Mrs. Grundy, you know. I love to dance, too; in fact, if it were not for my job I think I should abandon myself to pleasure. 'Tis not that I love jazz less but work more. I suspect that Hartley wrote this play to get good and even with me. He doesn't dance, you see, and last Summer I left him stranded and solitary so often at parties that he revenged himself in true husband fashion by writing this counterblast against jazz. And it worked! I'm cured!"

Confessedly, then, Laurette Taylor knows nothing about flappers. She doesn't even believe in flappers, though the eye of the world is full of them. I tried to hitch my wagon to another star.

Clothed in the mock majesty of "The Czarina" (Catharine the Great, no less), Doris Keane reclined on a chaise-longue in her dressing room at the Empire Theatre. Blame Miss Keane, not me, for the chaise-longue. It's old stuff, very old, dating back before Catharine's spacious time. But there it was and Miss Keane was on it.

"Why ask me about flappers?" said Mock Majesty. "I only know one flapper personally and she is my niece. Yes I seem to recall that they did jolly well in the war. In those days the cry was 'Hail the Young Girl!' Now it seems to be '*A bas* the flapper!'"

"I think the flapper is one hope of our stage today. Day in, day out, here in American the public get fed — and fed up — with pap — sugary, sloppy, sentimental plays; drama for the eight-year-old mind, I call it. The flapper won't stand for it, she passed that stage long ago. While her elders emote and weep all over the place she laughs. Hers is not a nervous, hysterical laugh, either. Heaven forbid! No! It is a superior supercilious chuckle betraying the right amount, just the fashionable amount, of amusement. In France theatre tickets for certain plays are marked '*Cette piece n'est pas pour les jeunes filles.*" No manager has dared do that in America. But soon we may have posters reading 'This Play for Flappers Only,' or 'Parents Admitted Only Accompanied by Flappers.'

"As Catharine in this piece I have to play an open-eyed woman of the world — very much of the world — to the star-eyed ingénue sentiment of the little lady-in-waiting — a little lady of flapper age but not of flapper quality. Today, Catharine of Russia and her little lady-in-waiting change changed placed; the femme du monde is now the ingénue and the young girl is the *femme du* — well, not quite that. I am sorry I don't know more about the sweet young things, but Art is a stern taskmistress. I don't see much of the world outside.

At that moment a maid entered, bearing on a dinner tray a frugal meal. "It is now what time?" asked Miss Keane.

"Five o'clock."

"What are your flappers doing now?"

"They are dancing, your Majesty."

"Ah!" and she sighed her best Czarina sigh. "Now you understand why I never see them. While they dance I dine, while they dine I rest from the play."

From which it may be argued — if you choose — that actresses in general, and Laurette Taylor and Doris Keane in particular, know little if anything about the world beyond the footlights. For them life is all work and no play, or all work and all "play," whichever way you look at it. For this reason it may be recorded (in the face of a shocked and amazed Dr. Straton) that actresses are among the old-fashionedest, the most conservative people in the world.

But if the flapper is an unknown quantity to the player, it is not so with the playwright. He knows her from tip to toe—the flippant, the idle flapper, the workaday flapper. Bernard Shaw discovered her early in the game. In fact, Shaw gets right at the heart of the flapper. For it is her fierce intensity, applied to work or play, ideas or art, which distinguishes her from the rest of her kind. Dolly in "You Never Can tell" was a flapper. So was Hypatia in "misalliance." In "Back to Methuselah" that very young person called Savvy is absorbed in world problems, savagely anxious to right the wrongs of the world, impatient of her long-winded conservative elders. Says she, eye to eye with a past and present Prime Mininsters of England:

"You know, Mr. Lubin, I am frightfully interested in the labor movement and in theosophy and in reconstruction after the war, and all sorts of things. I dare say the flappers in your smart set" (Laurette Taylor's flappers) "are tremendously flattered when you sit beside them and are nice to them, as you are being nice to me; but I am not smart; and I am no use as a flapper. I am dowdy and serious. I want you to be serious. If you refuse, I shall go and sit beside Mrs. Burge and ask him to hold my hand.

That her elders happen to be Mr. Lloyd George and Mr. Asquith only sharpens her biting tongue. Age and rank do not impress the flapper. You can't fool her. She may flap, but you can't feed her flapdoodle. (The dictionary definition reads "food for fools.") Man, whose stock in trade for centuries has been an assumption of mental superiority, deals with her at his peril. It is her game to spoil his high attitude.

The other night, at one of those crowded and exclusive all-night dancing places, a flapper was seated at a near-by table. In the same party was a well-known man, a personage of some consequence, and her senior by many years. Suddenly the flapper turned to him. "Good heavens! They told me you had brains. You must have, I suppose. What do you do with them? Do you 'park' them outside?"

The personage smiled, rather fatuously. He was not even annoyed.

"My success is now certain," he said. "A flapper doesn't want a man to have brains — she is three paces ahead of him, anyway, and a miss is as good as a mile. It is she who must do the choosing, or ordering about, the selecting — in fact, it would appear that we have got back but a circuitous route, to the biological axiom that the male is only incidental."

Nor is it only the elderly and the distinguished who fall for her. The young men also submit unresistingly to the flapper's rule. It is much less trouble, and then, of course, it invites the suspicion of being a boob or a rube to object. The young man's cue is to look bored and blasé, as if the newest woman were nothing new in his life. The prototype is in Townsend's famous cartoon in Punch, a cartoon showing what the English call a "nut" reclining languidly upon a couch and saying, "I don't bother with the girls. I just let 'em nestle."

Not on Broadway and Forty-second Street will you get the true picture of the flapper, and certainly not from conservative theatre folk, actresses and the like. For that you must go to the East Sixties. In the old home of Ledyard Blair, just off Fifth Avenue, you will find Miss Virginia Potter, President of the New York League of Girls Clubs, Inc. For forty years she has guided the fun and fortunes of thousands of young girls and Miss Potter is all for the flapper!

Hear her:

"I think the modern young girl is a delight. She dresses simply and sensibly, and she looks like right straight in the eye; she knows just what she wants and goes after it, whether it is a man, a career, a job or a new hat. Ten years ago the Chairman of our club was a young girl who had been brought up in an East Side tenement — a nice little girl. Her life was as carefully protected as that of any debutante here on Fifth Avenue. After school she played with her brothers and sisters in the back yard. Her mother wouldn't allow her to play in the streets. That would be impossible in 1922 — little daughter wouldn't stay in the back yard, even if mother tried to keep her there. The young girl of today has more sense than her grandmother had when she was young. I know, because I see thousands of them every year at our clubs. The mid-Victorian clinging vine has gone out, and I, for one, am glad of it.

Fifty years from now Miss Flapper of 1922 will sit in a box at the Charity Ball and her comment will run this way: "Isn't this too awful? The girls ask the young men for the dances, quite shamelessly, and the men accept timidly. And the fashions and conversations are shocking! My dear, in my day — well, we were not exactly shy, but — oh, this is terrible! My wrap, please! Yes, it is on that chair — thank you! Good evening!"

For your flapper of today is doomed to be the prude of tomorrow.

Flappers 'Merely Humans'

BY THE NEW YORK TIMES | MARCH 17, 1922

CHICAGO, MARCH 16 — There is nothing mysterious about the flapper — she is just "a female who has lived down thousands of years of hypocrisy and now has become what she most desired to be for ages, a human being," Dr. Lee A. Stone, head of the Chicago Department of Health, said today in an address before a health conference.

"Flapperism — or modern feminism — is just the revolt of youth," added Dr. Stone. "It is the resumption of the original status of mankind."

SOCIETY, SEX AND RELATIONSHIPS **189**

Asks Women Avoid Martyr Complex

BY DORIS GREENBERG | MAY 30, 1948

SYRACUSE, N.Y., MAY 29 — American women should abandon the notion that they are "martyrs" suffering unjust discriminations, Dr. M. Eunice Hilton, dean of women at Syracuse University, declared here today.

Speaking at one of the final sessions of the twenty-ninth annual convention of the Business and Professional Women's Clubs of New York State, she said that feminism was outdated.

Women must realize that men as well as women faced certain discriminations in modern society, Dean Hilton told 300 delegates and visitors attending the meeting.

Instead of placing continued emphasis on the restrictions affecting their own sex, she advised the club women to sponsor "co-ed" efforts to improve the lot of both sexes.

OLD FEMINIST IDEAS RECALLED

Referring to the coming celebration in Seneca Falls, N. Y., this summer of the centenary of the women's rights movement, Dean Hilton held that the feminist leaders who issued a declaration then terming men "tyrants" over women would be the first to recognize that times had since changed.

"The grave feminists of Seneca Falls — and I admire them all — who did us such a noble service unwittingly also did us a disservice," she added.

Their declaration, which was subsequently accepted as gospel by women everywhere, had tended to perpetuate the myth that women had been tyrannized by men throughout history, Dean Hilton contended.

She said that this thesis was patently untrue, as proved by the historian, Mrs. Mary Beard, in her book two years ago, "Women as a Force in History."

THESIS OF SUBJECTION HIT

Nevertheless, the idea was still widely held and it gave easy justification for the continuance of old discriminations and even the establishment of new one, she insisted.

"Have we, through a lack of knowledge of our own history, accepted too easily and too literally the thesis of subjection?" she asked.

"As a result, have we concentrated upon ourselves as a sex opposed to the masculine sex, fighting that sex, instead of as the feminine sex working with the masculine sex and recognizing that both groups have problems and bear discrimination in society?

"I believe that we have, and that we thus have developed a martyr complex for ourselves that inflates the ego of men and not only perpetuates discriminations, but makes for the creating of new ones."

Emphasizing that she did not mean to minimize the economic, social and political restraints still facing women, Dean Hilton said:

"But we can't feel sorry for ourselves any more."

There are just as many neurotic men as neurotic women in the confused world today, she asserted, "and statistics show that more men than women commit suicide."

Now the Booing is Done in Soprano

BY ALINE B. LOUCHHEIM | SEPT. 4, 1949

EVER SINCE A radio voice first droned, "The count is now three and two" into a kitchen, the number of "lady sports fans" has been increasing. But since the first television set dumped brawny wrestlers into the housewife's lap in her own living room, the increase has accelerated so much that a phenomenon has become an invasion.

This new feminine fervor varies, of course, from sport to sport. Pro football, tennis, ice-hockey and basketball all attract approximately twice as many women spectators as they did ten years ago. Prizefights appeal to about five times as many women fans on a nation-wide basis, but there is wide geographic variance in their interest. The ratio of females to males around the ringsides in the New York area is roughly one to seven; it is only one to twenty in Chicago. No one can explain why.

Baseball tops the list, however, by a wide margin. Executives of major league clubs agree that one hundred times as many women are interested in their game as were a decade ago. The "Oriels," a group of young matrons of assorted sizes and shapes who live in Oradel, N. J., are a case in point.

"We all have small kids," the giggling Oriel leader in a bright aqua dress explained. "Once a week we get a sitter for them. In the winter we go to theatre; in the summer to baseball." On one recent afternoon at the Polo Grounds, seven Oriels, all eating ice cream, sat in one row rooting for the Giants; seven others sat behind them cheering the opposing Brooklyn Dodgers. "Did you ever find fourteen women who could agree about anything?" one of the Giant-loving Oriels asked.

This increased interest of women in sports has given an indirect as well as a direct boost to the nation's box offices. In the old days when men went to sporting events alone, women often opposed the excursions. Now they approve of, and often even originate, them. Sports events are setting attendance records today partly because, like the movies and the theatre, they are now a form of co-educational entertainment.

Despite their recognition of women's importance to the gate, promoters have done very little to cater to the fair sex. "Ladies Day" exists only in baseball, and several promoters doubt if the institution makes any essential difference in the total picture. Radio, and more recently television, have done the conversion job.

Strikeouts have replaced the soap opera as the lesser of two afternoon radio evils for thousands of women listeners. For others, sports were an accidental discovery. Toots Shor, the owner of the famous restaurant, tells of the woman who was on top of a stepladder when the radio switched from Beethoven to baseball. By the time she had finished cleaning the chandelier and could descend to turn the dial it was the fourth inning and she was fascinated.

Radio has succeeded where patient males have failed. "You've got to learn baseball, you can't be taught," one exasperated husband remarked. But Mel Allen, Red Barber and the other announcers have done the impossible and explained the game to women.

Television has, of course, removed the last vestiges of athletic apathy. A husband who left his wife at home before TV cannot very well turn her out of the house when the Friday night bouts go on. And once she's had a look, the lady wants to see more.

The television cabinet has become a kind of Pandora's box which even the most bluestockinged female cannot resist, Jolting Joe. The Big Cat, Stan the Man become people rather than phantoms and nicknames for the video audience; the fine points of an uppercut are made vivid; through the camera eye the female fan can follow a football for the first time.

Proverbial feminine curiosity is teased. The TV cameras at the Polo Grounds, for instance, can pick up only the rear view of a left-handed batter. Intrigued by the nape of Whitey Lockman's neck and his very blond hair, a newly fledged Giant fan was at a game one day sitting behind third base so she could see the player's face when he batted. Another novice made the long trek to discover where the plate umpire kept his endless supply of baseballs.

The old chestnut is that women are the Dumb Doras who are as bothersome as mosquitos with their buzz of witless questions. There are, of course, still some of these wide-eyed gals in the athletic arenas. There are girls like the one who arrived belligerently at the Yankee Stadium for her first game demanding, "Well, where is he — the big guy — that Joe DiMaggio everyone talks about?" Her husband pointed patiently, "He's out there in center field where he always plays." "He is, is he?" The little lady flared. "Well, that's a darn shame. Most people here came to see Joe DiMaggio. Why doesn't he play up on the hill in the center so they can get a good look at him?"

And there are still some women who display more enthusiasm than knowledge. For instance, Jackie Farrell of the Yankees' publicity staff took his wife to a game one night, deposited her in a seat and ducked down under the stands to get her coffee and a hot dog. When he returned it was the second half of the inning and he noticed Yankee players on at first and second. "How did it happen? How did they get there?" he asked. "Well," his wife bubbled, "the first one ran like hell and the second one took his time." Only an inveterate fan could figure out that Stimweiss had hit a two-bagger and that Henrich had walked.

But most of the sports world agrees that women are now genuine fans. Sportswriters receive fewer crackpot letters from women than from men. In a seven-week Yankee-player identification program on WINS, the female contingent claimed 75 per cent of the 2,800 answers and three out of seven prizes.

But if a vast number of women fans are becoming as informed and intelligent as their male counterpart, they still betray their feminism by their violent vocalism and easy excitement. One is not surprised that the hardly reticent Tallulah Bankhead admits she lets out "a Comanche howl that can be heard from the Polo Grounds to Spuyten Duyvil." And that dignified lady of the theatre, Ethel Barrymore, was barred from radio rebroadcasts of ball games (which she used to attend on matinee days) because her fiendish screams drowned out the announcer.

At basketball games it is the female of the species which badgers visiting teams with epithets of "cry baby" and "sissy pants" and (especially in Fort Wayne, Tex.) the ladies who throw peanuts and pennies on the court when they get riled.

Despite traditional squeamishness, the gentler sex is credited by many observers with being more sadistic than the stronger one, secretly more delighted by a gory eye at a prize fight or a vicious tackle on the football field. Many women actually admit they like ice hockey because the boys are playing with potentially dangerous weapons which they are not adverse to using. And Hatpin Mary, who edged to the ringside and jabbed her stiletto-like hatpin into a wrestler's rears in order to promote more violent activity, was after all a member of the weaker sex.

In their sports-side manners, women have their peculiar habits. They smoke nervously and continuously at sporting events and although their capacity for beer and soft drinks is less than that of men, their quotas of peanuts and ice cream are appreciably higher. Only occasionally do they indulge in such distaff-side activities as knitting. One elderly lady, however, clicked her needles constantly in a center-court seat at Madison Square Garden basketball games last winter.

Women sport fans confirm a long-held male contention of the difference between the sexes; namely, that women are more concerned with personalities than principles, with the personal rather than the abstract. For it is true that almost all women are interested in the play in terms of the players.

For most women this is just a kind of "human interest" curiosity. It may lead to inquisitive mail about marital and parental status, off-season activities and likes and dislikes from food to phonograph records. Or it may swell the already voluminous demands for photographs.

Frequently women's interest in the players is maternal in nature. When Joe DiMaggio's left heel kept him out of play at the beginning of this season, his fan mail averaged over 400 letters a day. Over half of these were from women and an enormous number suggested remedies — from Epsom Salts baths to fat-free diets to bird-seed poultices.

For one segment of female fans, however, player-curiosity is more complex and less healthy. It seems to confirm what psychologists have also inferred from the popularity of Hollywood, women's magazines, soap operas and crooners: that many women — frustrated or unhappy or insecure or bored — live in a dream¬world peopled by unattainable Adonis-Hercules men.

The bobby-soxers "drool" outside dressing rooms waiting for autographs. According to several athletes, the girls grown to full-length nylons tuck mash notes under hotel room doors. The psycopathic girl who shot the Phillies' Eddie Waitkus because she "loved" him is, fortunately a unique "fan." But the adoration of others often crosses the sanity line.

Women are attracted by the physical appearance of the male athletes. One member of a pro basketball team said that many girls like his game "because the players aren't all covered up with heavy uniforms and equipment." A New York taxi-driver remarked perceptively to a male passenger one day, "You know the way we used to sneak off to the burlesque show, bud? Well, it's that way with my wife and wrestling."

Favorite players are usually those who are both proficient and attractive. One Chicago housewife who stormed into the Cubs' office announcing that she was going to sue because a home-run ball had broken a window in her near-by apartment was immediately pacified when she was told the batter had been handsome Billy Nicholson.

Even though they admit there is a difference in their attitude and actions, women fans defend their mass immigration into the sports world as another example of equal rights. Just as she has learned to stand in a bus and sit at a bar, the woman is convinced that she should be allowed her place not as a "lady fan" but as a "fan" in the sports world. Her passport, she believes, is the fact that she has learned the game and follows it ardently.

There are, of course, a few die-hard misogynists among male fans who tenaciously hold to the theory that the sports world is a man's world and should be as exclusively male as a Trappist monastery.

Some male fans face the inevitable — but not without misgivings. Arthur Daley of The Times tells of the man in Pittsburgh who wrote for tickets for the first night ball game ever held in the Smoky City. "Please send me two tickets," his letter read. "My wife has been working hard and deserves a rest, so I said she could go. But I've been working hard and deserve a rest, too, so please make one seat behind first base and one seat behind third."

On the whole, however, male fans have accepted the inroad into their world and actually enjoy the company of the lady fan — that is, if she has found and hews to that difficult line of avoiding foolish questions yet being careful not to know too much. The male still believes in his superior knowledge of sports and even if every day becomes ladies' day, the wise woman will nurture his illusion.

ALINE B. LOUCHHEIM, ASSOCIATE ART EDITOR OF THE NEW YORK TIMES, IS PARTICULARLY FOND OF THE ARTISTRY OF THE NEW YORK YANKEES.

Study Finds College Girl Weds Later

BY JOAN COOK | JUNE 1, 1964

PARENTS CONCERNED over the possibility of the daughter of the house impulsively plunging into an early marriage can take a tip from the Population Reference Bureau and get her into college fast. According to a new survey of marriage trends made by the Washington organization, a college career delays a girl's marriage four years.

The bureau reports that this year there will be about 1.8 million marriages in the United States. Some 220,000 brides are expected to say "I do" this month alone, the majority of whom will be teen-agers. Their bridegrooms will be only slightly older, the bureau reports.

Brides and bridegrooms in this country are younger and closer in age at first marriage, according to the bureau, than those in any other major urban-industrial country in the world. American age-at-marriage pattern — more women marry at 18 than at any other age, more men at 21 — now is closer to the Asian than the European.

OTHER FINDINGS

The bureau also discovered that:

Of the 596,300 students who make up the college class of 1964, approximately 38 per cent are women.

Women will receive almost 40 per cent of the bachelor's and first professional degrees, a third of the master's degrees, but only 11 per cent of the doctoral degrees.

Undergraduate marriage in the major colleges — a cause for expulsion a generation ago — is taboo only in the academies of the armed services.

Almost one-fourth of all students who will graduate this year are already married; another 13 per cent of June graduates expect to marry before the summer's end.

Four out of five married graduates are men. The dearth of women reflects, in part, the fact that many co-eds who marry drop out of college to bolster the family exchequer, often making it possible for husbands to graduate.

MARRIAGE AGES

The most frequent age at marriage for women college graduates is 22; for high school graduates, 18; for women who did not attend high school, 14 to 16.

Many married co-eds continue their studies on a part-time basis: 44 per cent of all part-time co-eds are married while only 5 per cent of full-time co-eds have husbands.

Among married women, a larger proportion of college graduates than high school graduates has jobs.

A college degree is a passport to better jobs. Of all women with an income, only 6 per cent received more than $5,000, according to the 1960 census. Twenty-four per cent of women college graduates had an income of over $5,000, as did 45 per cent of those who had completed some graduate work.

The college dropout ratio is the same for both sexes — four out of every ten who enter. Among women, marriage is most frequently given as the reason for leaving school.

National Survey Finds The Sexual Harassing Of Students Is Rising

BY THE NEW YORK TIMES | OCT. 12, 1980

WASHINGTON, OCT. 11 (UPI) — A survey released today said that sexual harassment of students was showing up more frequently and should be treated as a form of illegal discrimination.

The National Advisory Council on Women's Education, which was appointed by the President, issued a report saying that sexual harassment of students violated Federal law prohibiting discrimination in federally financed education programs.

The council recommended that the Education Department's civil rights office "explicitly establish sexual harassment as a sex-based discrimination," and called on all Federal agencies, colleges and universities to "reduce tolerance for sexual harassment on the campus."

"Victims usually feel isolated and try to cope with even severe sexual harassment on their own," said Susan Vance, council chairman. She said, "Only a few institutions have adequate mechanisms for dealing with this increasingly visible problem."

In many circumstances, the council found that victims could file charges under state and Federal non-discrimination laws or bring criminal or civil suits against both the school and the harassing party.

The council defined five categories of sexual harassment:

• General sexist remarks or behavior that, the council found, was "closest in appearance to racial harassment directed at the victim because of her (or his) gender," and possibly including suggestive jokes and stories and crudely sexual remarks.

• Inappropriate and offensive, but essentially sanction-free sexual advances that could include a sexual proposition by an instructor toward a student.

• Solicitation of sexual activity or other sex-related behavior by promise of rewards. The panel said such activity could include threats and might "in its most blatant forms be prosecuted as a criminal act."

• Coercion of sexual activity by threat of punishment.

• Sexual crimes and misdemeanors. "For the most part," the council said, "they go unreported, even when they are extreme — such as forced sexual intercourse — because of a student-victim's fear of reporting the incidents to any authority."

Voices of the New Generation; Date Rape Hysteria

BY KATIE ROIPHE | NOV. 20, 1991

IN CLASSROOMS and journals, in lectures and coffee shops, academics everywhere are talking about rape. Although it wears a fashionable leftist mask, this is a neo-puritan preoccupation. While real women get battered, while real mothers need day care, certain feminists are busy turning rape into fiction. Every time one Henry James character seizes the hand of another Henry James character, someone is calling it rape.

At a certain point the metaphor gets paranoid. An overused word, like an over-painted sunset, becomes a cliche, drained of specificity and meaning. With every new article on rape imagery, we threaten to confirm the vision of that 18th-century patriarch, Henry Fielding, when he wrote, "These words of exclamation (murder! robbery! rape!) are used by ladies in a fright, as fa la la … are in music, only as vehicles of sound and without any fixed idea."

Only now the cry across campuses is "date rape." Those involved frame it as a liberal concern, cut and dry, beyond debate. But they don't stop to consider the fundamentally sexist images lurking beneath their rhetoric. The term "date rape" itself hints at its conservative bent. More than just a polemic against rape, it reveals a desire for dates.

Although not an explicit part of their movement, these feminists are responding, in this time of sexual suspicion, to the need for a more rigid courtship structure. The message represents, in part, a nostalgia for 1950s-style dating. For Johnny picking Susie up for a movie and a Coke.

And the assumption embedded in this movement is our grandmother's assumption: men want sex, women don't. In emphasizing this struggle, him pushing, her resisting, the movement against date rape recycles and promotes an old model of sexuality.

One book, "Avoiding Rape On and Off Campus," by Carol Pritchard, warns young women to "think carefully before you go to a male friend's apartment or dorm …. Do not expose yourself to any unnecessary risk." When did the possibility of sex become an "unnecessary risk"? Are we really such fragile creatures that we need such an extreme definition of safety? Should we really subject our male friends to scrutiny because after all men want one thing and one thing only?

The definition of date rape stretches beyond acts of physical force. According to pamphlets widely distributed on college campuses, even "verbal coercion" constitutes "date rape." With this expansive version of rape, then, these feminists invent a kinder, gentler sexuality. These pamphlets are clearly intended to protect innocent college women from the insatiable force of male desire. We have been hearing about this for centuries. He is still nearly uncontrollable; she is still the one drawing lines. This so-called feminist movement peddles an image of gender relations that denies female desire and infantilizes women. Once again, our bodies seem to be sacred vessels. We've come a long way, and now it seems, we are going back.

The date rape pamphlets begin to sound like Victorian guides to conduct. The most common date rape guide, published by the American College Health Association, advises its delicate readers to "communicate your limits clearly. If someone starts to offend you, tell them firmly and early."

Sharing these assumptions about female sensibilities, a manners guide from 1853 advises young women, "Do not suffer your hand to be held or squeezed without showing that it displeases you by instantly withdrawing it …. These and many other little points of refinement will operate as an almost invisible though a very impenetrable fence, keeping off vulgar familiarity, and that desecration of the person which has so often led to vice." And so ideals of female virtue and repression resonate through time.

Let's not chase the same stereotypes our mothers have spent so much energy running away from. Let's not reinforce the images that oppress us, that label us victims, and deny our own agency and intelligence, as strong and sensual, as autonomous, pleasure-seeking, sexual beings.

On Campus, Embracing Feminism and Facing the Future

BY EILENE ZIMMERMAN | MARCH 31, 2017

ONE OF THE THINGS Tina Campt, a professor and director of the Barnard Center for Research on Women, has noticed about the young women in her classes is their radically open notion of sexuality and gender.

"These students want the freedom to express who they are without the constraints of choices such as either a woman or man, heterosexual or homosexual," Dr. Campt said. "Those categories no longer carry a definitional value."

Women now account for the majority of college students, according to the National Center for Education Statistics, 11.3 million of them as compared with 8.7 million men. And 63 percent identify as feminist. Their concerns run the gamut, from sexual assault and poverty to affordable education, immigration and reproductive rights, said Alison Dahl Crossley, the associate director of the Clayman Institute for Gender Research at Stanford University.

Both Dr. Campt and Dr. Crossley, who is also author of the book "Finding Feminism: Millennial Activists and the Unfinished Gender Revolution," say women today are in a world that is profoundly different from what it was a generation ago, so they are having to create ways of coping with new challenges, the same as previous generations did.

"The structure of the economy, of family and of work is very, very different," Dr. Campt said.

She said young women today were entering an economy with fewer work opportunities and much more debt. It is also an era in which feminist activism and education happen in both the physical world and the virtual one, often through blogs and social media.

One thing that surprised Dr. Crossley about the college women she studied was their wholehearted embrace of feminism. "They spoke

KATHERINE TAYLOR FOR THE NEW YORK TIMES

The Crimson Women's Coalition protested at Harvard after the university announced restrictions on members of single-sex organizations.

about how feminism permeated their worldview and their interactions and the relationships they had in their everyday lives," she said.

We spoke to female undergraduates at colleges around the country to find out what issues they were most concerned about and what feminism meant to them. Their comments have been edited and condensed.

MORGAN BROWNLEE, 22
Graduated from San Diego State University in December; Sociology major and French minor

The biggest issue for me as a woman on campus is safety and acceptance. When I walk in a room, I do a quick scan to see if there are any other women there. And if there are men, I look at how many are white, and their ages. It gives me a sense of the openness of the room.

I worry about equality of pay, and it's something that when I hear my dad talk about, as a black man, I think, "He'll still probably make more than I ever will," because not only am I a woman, but I'm black.

I feel like the women's movement doesn't represent women of color as well as it could. I'm not expecting the movement to be perfect, but if you're talking about women earning 80 cents for every dollar a man makes, you're not really talking about Latina women, black women, Native American women, who make even less than that.

MELANIE CAMEJO COFFIGNY, 18
First-Year Student, Duke University; Neuroscience major

If you had asked me my concerns about being a woman six months ago, I don't know if they would have been the same. The election and college have changed that. I'm a Cuban immigrant — I came to the U.S. in 2009, when I was 11 years old — and what concerns me most now is the idea of safety, both on the college campus and in the world.

I'm very involved with the fight against rape culture, and I'm out as an L.G.B.T. student and activist. But the climate in North Carolina now, that's something to be concerned about.

I worry a lot about immigration status. I'm technically safe, but who knows what will happen now. The whole idea of safety as something that is given to us by society concerns me. The idea that we are to blame for what happens to us — women, minorities, immigrants — because of how we dress or express ourselves or our immigration status. There's so much victim-blaming.

I consider myself a feminist, and that means attaining equality in all the senses that entails. As an out woman of color, it's the idea that I will be able to be myself and fight for the things I care about.

ALEXA DANTZLER, 21
Senior, Emory University, Atlanta; Biology and African studies major

For me as a woman, what I see on campus and in the bigger world is that we're always fighting for equal opportunity and access. I am on the pre-med track, and I'm also African-American, Korean and Slovak. I see such a lack of minority women in STEM.

I haven't had a physician mentor who is a minority woman, and I think it's harder to relate to role models in your future career field when they haven't had the same racial experiences. I don't have someone I can ask: "What was it like being a black woman in your medical school classes? What were the challenges you faced?" That's a real concern of mine.

On campus, I'm concerned about the language and rhetoric used to describe minority groups, and that includes women. I think our voices may be heard less as a result of the current rhetoric and the direct implications of it.

LEXI HOAGLAND, 20

Sophomore, Harding University, Searcy, Ark.; Public relations and marketing major

I'm concerned that some women don't feel capable of succeeding or comfortable in our own skin. I am a conservative Christian and my morals and beliefs line up with that, but I would also say I'm a conservative Christian feminist. I believe in God and I am definitely pro-woman, but I'm also pro-man.

I believe God created men and created women with different skills and talents to serve for different reasons. Feminism to me is believing in myself, following my dreams and empowering other people — both men and women.

There's a scripture in the Bible that I fall back on a lot, that I aspire to live by, and it's really important. In Proverbs 31, it talks about being a "wife of noble character." I'm not married, but I take it to mean not a wife but rather a woman of noble character. Full of confidence in myself and bringing good to everyone around me, being a hard and persistent worker, being respectful, being bold — not shrinking or weak.

KAT KERWIN, 19
Sophomore, University of Wisconsin, Madison; Political science and
geography major

The biggest issue on campus for women here is sexual assault, being afraid of the young men we know here, who are in our lives.

One of my best friends was sexually assaulted a year ago but didn't report it, and we were out at a bar and he was there. She was very uncomfortable with him being there, and I went up to him and said, "Look, she feels really uncomfortable, could you leave?" He said no. It's concerning, the rape culture and lack of respect for women.

Another big concern for me as a woman is being able to graduate and find a job. I think as a woman it's a lot more difficult. Guys are given priority — you've seen the studies where if it says you're a man on your résumé you are more likely to get hired. I'm also bothered that if you're an assertive woman — and I'm called aggressive all the time simply because I'm assertive — it's misconstrued as bossiness. That really undermines us. It says to women it's not O.K. for us to be driven, ambitious and have strong opinions.

KELSEY RITCHIE, 22,
Senior, Texas Christian University, Fort Worth; Political science and journalism major, business minor

I am concerned about unequal pay between men and women in the workplace. I'm going to grad school after college to study public policy and if I have debt after that, will I be able to pay it off as well as my male peers? Because men earn more. When I look at jobs, I know it will take me X amount of years longer to pay off my school debt than it would if I were a man. That could affect my ability to pursue a career I'm passionate about.

I consider myself a feminist and also a pretty religious Christian. I went to the march in Washington this past January, but I also went to the inauguration. I look at feminism as feeling empowered enough to behave in a way that demands respect, rather than acting in a way that demands attention. I am a student body vice president at T.C.U. and very career-focused. I've thought a lot about balancing what the world defines as a strong woman with biblical truths, such as this phrase in Scripture: "Submit to your husband."

The Bible is very clear about men being the ones to lead relationships. And for a long time it was difficult for me to accept this, but I've realized it doesn't have to demean a woman's role in a relationship. Submission doesn't have to come from weakness. We are all called to serve each other by utilizing our strengths. My biblical foundation empowers me to advocate for women's rights.

Glossary

abortion The intentional termination of a pregnancy.

activist One who campaigns to manifest social or political change.

advocate To publicly support or argue for a cause.

birth control The prevention of unwanted pregnancies.

blackguard A person who behaves in a rude, unscrupulous, or dishonorable way.

Bloomer costume A short skirt over loose pants gathered at the ankles, primarily worn in the 1850s, and named after Amelia Bloomer, who advocated a dress reform.

co-ed A female student at a co-educational institution.

date rape The rape of a victim by a perpetrator with whom the victim is acquainted.

debutante A young woman making a formal entrance into society, often with the purpose of meeting marriage prospects.

discrimination The unfair treatment of a person or group based on categorical differences like race, age, or sex.

empower To grant someone authority.

feminism The advocacy for rights on the grounds of political, social, and economic equality of the sexes.

flapper A young woman in the 1920s who flouted social and sexual norms by engaging in unconventional behavior, such as wearing short skirts, having short hair, listening to jazz, driving automobiles, and having casual sex.

gender The socially constructed characteristics of masculinity and femininity.

heady Having a strong and exhilarating effect.

housewife A married woman who primarily takes care of the household and family.

legislation A law or body of laws.

mansplain When a man explains, often in a condescending or patronizing manner, something to a woman of which he has less knowledge than she.

prejudice A preconceived opinion or judgment formed on insufficient grounds.

rape Sexual penetration without the victim's consent.

right A legal freedom or entitlement.

separatism The advocacy for a separation of one group from another on the basis of race, gender, religion, or other category.

sexism Discrimination or prejudice against women on the basis of gender.

sexual assault Unwanted sexual contact.

sine die Latin term meaning no set date for resumption, such as in the case of a meeting.

suffrage The right to vote.

Media Literacy Terms

"Media literacy" refers to the ability to access, understand, critically assess and create media. The following terms are important components of media literacy, and they will help you critically engage with the articles in this title.

angle The aspect of a news story on which a journalist focuses and develops.

attribution The method by which a source is identified or by which facts and information are assigned to the person who provided them.

balance Principle of journalism that both perspectives of an argument should be presented in a fair way.

chronological order Method of writing a story presenting the details of the story in the order in which they occurred.

commentary Type of story that is an expression of opinion on recent events by a journalist generally known as a commentator.

credibility The quality of being trustworthy and believable, said of a journalistic source.

critical review Type of story that describes an event or work of art, such as a theater performance, film, concert, book, restaurant, radio or television program, exhibition or musical piece, and offers critical assessment of its quality and reception.

editorial Article of opinion or interpretation.

feature story Article designed to entertain as well as to inform.

headline Type, usually 18 point or larger, used to introduce a story.

human interest story Type of story that focuses on individuals and how events or issues affect their lives, generally offering a sense of relatability to the reader.

impartiality Principle of journalism that a story should not reflect a journalist's bias and should contain balance.

intention The motive or reason behind something, such as the publication of a news story.

interview story Type of story in which the facts are gathered primarily by interviewing another person or persons.

motive The reason behind something, such as the publication of a news story or a source's perspective on an issue.

news story An article or style of expository writing that reports news, generally in a straightforward fashion and without editorial comment.

op-ed An opinion piece that reflects a prominent journalist's opinion on a topic of interest.

paraphrase The summary of an individual's words, with attribution, rather than a direct quotation of their exact words.

plagiarism An attempt to pass another person's work as one's own without attribution.

quotation The use of an individual's exact words indicated by the use of quotation marks and proper attribution.

reliability The quality of being dependable and accurate, said of a journalistic source.

rhetorical device Technique in writing intending to persuade the reader or communicate a message from a certain perspective.

source The origin of the information reported in journalism.

tone A manner of expression in writing or speech.

Media Literacy Questions

1. The article "The Question of Lady Doctors." (on page 72) contains two letters to the editor. Identify how the writers' attitudes, tones, and biases help convey their opinions on the topic.

2. Compare the headlines of "Equal Pay for Women" (on page 78) and "Women's Pay Gap Is Still Widening, U.S. Official Says" (on page 93). Which is a more compelling headline, and why? How could the less compelling headline be changed to better draw the reader's interest?

3. What type of story is "Reasessing Women's Political Role: The Lasting Impact of Geradline Ferraro" (on page 124)? Can you identify another article in this collection that is the same type of story?

4. "Female-Run Venture Capital Funds Alter the Status Quo" (on page 97) features multiple photographs. What do the photographs add to the article?

5. Does Nadine Brozan demonstrate the journalistic principle of balance and impartiality in her article "Men and Housework: Do They or Don't They?" (on page 54)? If so, how? If not, what could she have included to make her article more balanced and impartial?

6. "Money Is Power. And Women Need More of Both." (on page 166) features an illustration. What does this illustration add to the article?

7. Does "Push for Gender Equality in Tech? Some Men Say It's Gone Too Far" (on page 111) use multiple sources? What are the strengths of using multiple sources in a journalistic piece? What are the weaknesses of relying heavily on one source or few sources?

8. What is the intention of the article "More Ado About the Flapper" (on page 183)? How effectively does it achieve its intended purpose?

9. Compare the headlines of "The Women and the War." (on page 69) and "All Combat Roles Now Open to Women, Defense Secretary Says" (on page 103). Which is a more compelling headline, and why? How could the less compelling headline be changed to better draw the reader's interest?

10. What type of story is "Gertrude Jeannette, Actor, Director and Cabdriver, Dies at 103" (on page 86)? Can you identify another article in this collection that is the same type of story?

11. "Where Is Women's Place?" (on page 52) is an example of a critical review. What is the purpose of a critical review? Do you feel this article achieved that purpose?

12. Identify the various sources cited in the article "When the Pilot Is a Mom: Accommodating New Motherhood at 30,000 Feet" (on page 108). How does the journalist attribute information to each of these sources in her article? How effective are her attributions in helping the reader identify her sources?

Citations

All citations in this list are formatted according to the Modern Language Association's (MLA) style guide.

BOOK CITATION

THE NEW YORK TIMES EDITORIAL STAFF. *Women's Roles*. New York: New York Times Educational Publishing, 2019.

ARTICLE CITATIONS

BARNARD, EUNICE FULLER. "Women's Place: Home or Office?" *The New York Times,* 10 Aug. 1930, https://timesmachine.nytimes.com/timesmachine/1930/08/10/140605422.pdf.

BENNHOLD, KATRIN. "A Man Among Female Leaders: 'The Risk of Mansplaining Is Very High.' " *The New York Times,* 2 Dec. 2017, https://www.nytimes.com/2017/12/02/world/europe/iceland-gender-equality-women-political-leaders.html.

BOWLES, NELLIE. "Push for Gender Equality in Tech? Some Men Say It's Gone Too Far." *The New York Times,* 23 Sep. 2017, https://www.nytimes.com/2017/09/23/technology/silicon-valley-men-backlash-gender-scandals.html.

BROZAN, NADINE. "Men and Housework: Do They or Don't They?" *The New York Times,* 1 Nov. 1980, https://timesmachine.nytimes.com/timesmachine/1980/11/01/112164258.html.

CAIN MILLER, CLAIRE. "Female-Run Venture Capital Funds Alter the Status Quo." *The New York Times,* 1 Apr. 2015, https://www.nytimes.com/2015/04/02/business/dealbook/female-run-venture-funds-alter-the-status-quo.html.

CHIRA, SUSAN. "Money Is Power. And Women Need More of Both." *The New York Times,* 10 Mar. 2018, https://www.nytimes.com/2018/03/10/sunday-review/women-money-politics-power.html.

CHOZICK, AMY. "Hillary Clinton Ignited a Feminist Movement. By Losing." *The*

New York Times, 13 Jan. 2018, https://www.nytimes.com/2018/01/13/
sunday-review/hillary-clinton-feminist-movement.html.

COLLINS, GAIL. "Donald Trump's Gift to Women." *The New York Times,* 13 Dec.
2017, https://www.nytimes.com/2017/12/13/opinion/donald-trump-women.html.

COOK, JOAN. "Study Finds College Girl Weds Later." *The New York Times,*
1 Jun. 1964, https://www.nytimes.com/1964/06/01/study-finds-college-girl
-weds-later.html.

DOWD, MAUREEN. "Reassessing Women's Political Role: The Lasting Impact of
Geraldine Ferraro." *The New York Times,* 30 Dec. 1984, https://www
.nytimes.com/1984/12/30/magazine/reassessing-women-s-political-role
-the-lasting-impact-of-geraldine-ferraro.html.

FORTIN, JACEY. "She Was the Only Woman in a Photo of 38 Scientists, and
Now She's Been Identified." *The New York Times,* 19 Mar. 2018, https://
www.nytimes.com/2018/03/19/us/twitter-mystery-photo.html.

GOLDSTEIN, RICHARD. "Rose Gacioch, a Star in Women's Pro Baseball, Dies
at 89." *The New York Times,* 16 Sept 2004, https://www.nytimes.com/2004/
09/16/sports/baseball/rose-gacioch-a-star-in-womens-pro-baseball-dies
-at-89.html.

GREENBERG, DORIS. "Asks Women Avoid Martyr Complex." *The New York
Times,* 30 May 1948, https://timesmachine.nytimes.com/timesmachine/
1948/05/30/85262658.html.

GRUNWALD, BEVERLY. "Where Is Women's Place?" *The New York Times,* 9
Aug 1964, https://www.nytimes.com/1964/08/09/archives/where-is-womens
-place-after-nora-slammed-the-door-american-women-in.html.

INGALLS, LEONARD. "Women's Job Bill Fought in Albany" *The New York Times,*
14 Mar 1964, https://www.nytimes.com/1964/03/14/archives/womens-job
-bill-fought-in-albany-businesses-opposed-to-ban-on.html.

JOHNSON, JULIE. "2 Approaches to Rebuilding Women's Movement." *The New
York Times,* Aug. 14 1989, https://www.nytimes.com/1989/08/14/us/
washington-talk-2-approaches-to-rebuilding-women-s-movement.html.

KURZ, ANNALYN. "When the Pilot Is a Mom: Accommodating New Motherhood
at 30,000 Feet." *The New York Times,* 16 Aug. 2016, https://www.nytimes
.com/2016/08/17/business/when-the-captain-is-mom-accommodating-new
-motherhood-at-30000-feet.html.

LEWIN, TAMAR. "Guiding the Battles of the Women's Rights Movement." *The
New York Times,* 16 Dec. 2000, https://www.nytimes.com/2000/12/16/us/
public-lives-guiding-the-battles-of-the-women-s-rights-movement.html.

LEWIN, TAMAR. "More Women Find Room for Babies and Advanced Degrees." *The New York Times,* 7 May 2015, https://www.nytimes.com/2015/05/08/ us/more-highly-educated-women-are-also-having-children-researchers -find.html.

LEWIN, TAMAR. "More Young Women Waiting to Leave Home." *The New York Times,* 11 Nov. 2015, https://www.nytimes.com/2015/11/12/us/more-young -women-waiting-to-leave-home.html.

LOUCHHEIM, ALINE B. "Now the Booing is Done in Soprano." *The New York Times,* 4 Sept. 1949, https://timesmachine.nytimes.com/timesmachine/ 1949/09/04/93327292.html.

MADDEN, RICHARD L. "Mrs. Chisholm Defeats Farmer, Is First Negro Woman in House." *The New York Times,* 6 Nov. 1968, https://timesmachine.nytimes .com/timesmachine/1968/11/06/91291879.pdf.

MATHER, VICTOR. "An Olympic Figure Skater Who Also Made History for The Times." *The New York Times,* 21 Feb. 2018, https://www.nytimes.com/2018/ 02/21/insider/olympic-figure-skater-first-female-sportswriter-for-the-times .html.

MITCHELL, ALISON. "To Understand Clinton's Moment, Consider That It Came 32 Years After Ferraro's." *The New York Times,* 11 Jun. 2016, https://www .nytimes.com/2016/06/12/us/politics/women-white-house-clinton-geraldine -ferraro.html.

THE NEW YORK TIMES. "Call to Action." *The New York Times,* 24 Mar. 1972, https://www.nytimes.com/1972/03/24/archives/call-to-action.html.

THE NEW YORK TIMES. "Equal Pay for Women." *The New York Times,* 11 Nov. 1916, https://timesmachine.nytimes.com/timesmachine/1916/11/12/100340414 .pdf.

THE NEW YORK TIMES. "Flappers 'Merely Human.' " *The New York Times,* 17 Mar. 1922, https://timesmachine.nytimes.com/timesmachine/1922/03/ 17/99000102.pdf.

THE NEW YORK TIMES. "It is Not a Woman's Right." *The New York Times,* 16 Dec. 1852, https://timesmachine.nytimes.com/timesmachine/1852/12/16/ 75123353.html.

THE NEW YORK TIMES. "John P. Hale on Women's Rights." *The New York Times,* 17 July 1858, https://timesmachine.nytimes.com/timesmachine/ 1858/07/17/78857006.pdf.

THE NEW YORK TIMES. "Legislation for Women." *The New York Times,* 27 July 1857, https://timesmachine.nytimes.com/timesmachine/1857/07/28/

78503000.pdf.

THE NEW YORK TIMES. "Mrs. Sanger Defies Courts Before 3,000." *The New York Times,* 30 Jan. 1917, https://timesmachine.nytimes.com/timesmachine/1917/01/30/102315952.pdf.

THE NEW YORK TIMES. "National Survey Finds The Sexual Harassing Of Students Is Rising." *The New York Times,* 12 Oct. 1980, https://timesmachine.nytimes.com/timesmachine/1980/10/12/114142173.pdf.

THE NEW YORK TIMES. "The Old Wife and the New." *The New York Times,* 19 Sept. 1897, https://timesmachine.nytimes.com/timesmachine/1897/09/19/102062403.pdf.

THE NEW YORK TIMES. "The Question of Lady Doctors." *The New York Times,* 8 Jan. 1865, https://www.nytimes.com/1865/01/08/archives/the-question-of-lady-doctors.html.

THE NEW YORK TIMES. "Senators Back Amendment On Equal Rights for Women." *The New York Times,* 12 Sept. 1964, https://www.nytimes.com/1964/09/12/archives/senators-back-amendment-on-equal-rights-for-women.html.

THE NEW YORK TIMES. "Shall Wives Be Wage Earners?" *The New York Times,* 24 Sept. 1906, https://timesmachine.nytimes.com/timesmachine/1906/09/24/101799194.pdf.

THE NEW YORK TIMES. "Suffrage Wins in Senate; Now Goes to States." *The New York Times,* 4 Jun. 1919, https://timesmachine.nytimes.com/timesmachine/1919/06/05/97092194.pdf.

THE NEW YORK TIMES. "A Woman's Opinion." *The New York Times,* 17 Oct. 1898, https://timesmachine.nytimes.com/timesmachine/1898/10/17/102569102.pdf.

THE NEW YORK TIMES. "Woman's Place the Home." *The New York Times,* 17 Oct. 1898, https://timesmachine.nytimes.com/timesmachine/1904/05/06/118945552.pdf.

THE NEW YORK TIMES. "Woman's Rights." *The New York Times,* 18 Oct. 1851, https://timesmachine.nytimes.com/timesmachine/1851/10/18/87822606.pdf.

THE NEW YORK TIMES. "The Women and the War." *The New York Times,* 3 Aug. 1862, https://www.nytimes.com/1862/08/03/archives/the-women-and-the-war.html.

THE NEW YORK TIMES. "Women Greet Miss Rankin." *The New York Times,* 3 Apr. 1917, https://timesmachine.nytimes.com/timesmachine/1917/04/03/102328215.pdf.

THE NEW YORK TIMES. "Women's Pay Gap Is Still Widening, U. S. Official Says." *The New York Times,* 16 Nov. 1964, https://www.nytimes.com/1964/

11/16/archives/womens-pay-gap-is-still-widening-us-official-says.html.

THE NEW YORK TIMES. "Women's Rights Convention." *The New York Times,* 5 Jun. 1852, https://timesmachine.nytimes.com/timesmachine/1852/06/05/87835153.pdf.

O'LEARY, MARGARET. "More Ado about the Flapper." *The New York Times,* 16 Apr. 1922, https://timesmachine.nytimes.com/timesmachine/1922/04/16/107051068.pdf.

PETERSEN, ANNE. "Women Fitting Themselves Fast for Skilled Jobs in War Plants." *The New York Times,* 6 Sept. 1942, https://timesmachine.nytimes.com/timesmachine/1942/09/06/85048624.pdf.

PHILIPPS, DAVE, AND MATTHEW ROSENBERG. "All Combat Roles Now Open to Women, Defense Secretary Says." *The New York Times,* 3 Dec. 2015, https://www.nytimes.com/2015/12/04/us/politics/combat-military-women-ash-carter.html.

ROIPHE, KATIE. "Voices of the New Generation; Date Rape Hysteria." *The New York Times,* 20 Nov. 1991, https://www.nytimes.com/1991/11/20/opinion/voices-of-the-new-generation-date-rape-hysteria.html.

RUBIN, NANCY. "Women Who Mean Business." *The New York Times,* 12 Oct. 1980, https://timesmachine.nytimes.com/timesmachine/1980/10/12/114145370.html.

STOCKMAN, FARAH. "One Year After Women's March, More Activism but Less Unity." *The New York Times,* 15 Jan. 2018, https://www.nytimes.com/2018/01/15/us/womens-march-anniversary.html.

SWARNS, RACHEL L. "Considering the Place of the Working Parent in the Kitchen." *The New York Times,* 16 Nov. 2014, https://www.nytimes.com/2014/11/17/nyregion/considering-the-place-of-the-working-parent-in-the-kitchen.html.

TAUB, AMANDA. "How Should We Respond to Sexual Harassment?" *The New York Times,* 29 Nov. 2017, https://www.nytimes.com/2017/11/29/upshot/sexual-harassment-response-legal-system-guidelines.html.

WOLFE, JONATHAN. "Gertrude Jeannette, Actor, Director and Cabdriver, Dies at 103." *The New York Times,* 26 Apr. 2018, https://www.nytimes.com/2018/04/26/obituaries/gertrude-jeannette-actor-director-and-cabdriver-dies-at-103.html.

ZIMMERMAN, EILENE. "On Campus, Embracing Feminism and Facing the Future." *The New York Times,* 31 Mar. 2017, https://www.nytimes.com/2017/03/31/us/on-campus-embracing-feminism-and-facing-the-future.html.

Index

3 1333 04989 5079